A LITTLE OFF.
ALWAYS ON.

A LITTLE OFF.
ALWAYS ON.

A MEMOIR

MORA BRINKMAN

NEW DEGREE PRESS
COPYRIGHT © 2023 MORA BRINKMAN
All rights reserved.

A LITTLE OFF. ALWAYS ON.
A Memoir

ISBN   979-8-88926-925-0 *Paperback*
        979-8-88926-968-7 *Ebook*

Cover illustration by Frankie Oviedo

For my husband, David.

*I felt like I belonged once I met you.
Thanks for always letting me be me.*

CONTENTS

AUTHOR'S NOTE		9
INTRODUCTION		11
CHAPTER 1.	LEFT, LEFT, LEFT WHEN OTHERS ARE RIGHT	19
CHAPTER 2.	PHYSICAL EDUCATION	33
CHAPTER 3.	LITTLE MEN	51
CHAPTER 4.	TEAM SPORTS	61
CHAPTER 5.	SUPERWOMAN	75
CHAPTER 6.	MAKING HISTORY	87
CHAPTER 7.	LATE BLOOMER	103
CHAPTER 8.	HOMETOWN INTERN	119
CHAPTER 9.	KEEPING UP WITH THE SAMANTHA JONESES	129
CHAPTER 10.	THE JEFFERSON HOUSE	143
CHAPTER 11.	THE PLAN	155
CHAPTER 12.	CONCLUSION	171
ACKNOWLEDGMENTS		175
APPENDIX		179

AUTHOR'S NOTE

This book is a combination of facts about my life and certain embellishments. The events in this book are true and retold to the best of my recollection. While the spirit and tone of the dialogue reflect what occurred, it is not word for word. Some names, identifying circumstances, and details were changed to protect people's privacy.

INTRODUCTION

Recently, I found a college journal while cleaning my childhood bedroom. In a small book bound in a dramatic blue-and-pink paisley cloth, I had cataloged my finals, lamented saying goodbye to friends after graduation, wrote bad poetry about my broken heart, and made tidy lists of future goals. One list, in particular, caught my eye.

Before I went to graduate school, I sat cross-legged in a booth at the first Starbucks in Springfield, Missouri, and sipped my latte hack—a Caffè Misto, which was steamed milk and coffee—because espresso was too expensive. There, at the ripe age of twenty-two, wearing my favorite boot-cut jeans and gray Gap hoodie, I wrote the list titled, "Forty Goals by Forty Years Old."

In heavy-inked cursive, I wrote specific expectations and hopes for the future. Some items seemed standard while others were weirdly specific. The list was as follows:

1. Marry a man I love and like.
2. Earn a master's degree.
3. Have at least one child.

4. Have a career that uses my degrees (journalism, public relations, advertising).
5. Purchase a piece of art from a gallery or auction, *framed*, just because I like it.
6. Live in or near a major metropolitan city.
7. Live near or have access to a large body of water (an ocean or lake).
8. Pay off school loans.
9. Write something and have it published or printed (professionally—Kinkos doesn't count).
10. Host Thanksgiving or Christmas dinner for my family and friends.
11. Try French perfumes and choose one that is me. Establish a "signature scent."
12. Live close to my family. So close that we can make brunch for each other and it's not a big deal.
13. Learn to ride a horse. Jumps are preferred, not mandatory.
14. Own a traditional, cozy home and put down roots.
15. Have a dog. They make life better.
16. Lose thirty pounds. (This amount may change and will be reevaluated closer to age forty.)
17. Talk about wine without sounding like an idiot.
18. Speak conversational Spanish.
19. Travel Europe by train.
20. Finish *The Fountainhead*.
21. Start *War and Peace*.
22. Trace my ancestry.
23. Find a type of exercise I enjoy.
24. Travel somewhere outside my comfort zone.
25. Pay off credit cards.

26. Master creating beachy waves with my straightening iron.
27. Drink eight glasses of water a day.
28. Invest in skin care. Moisturize. SPF every day.
29. Have a signature dessert for gatherings and events.
30. Attend mass regularly.
31. Work at a global company.
32. Support working artists (with reasonable egos).
33. Join a choir.
34. Live in a different country.
35. Support a charity regularly.
36. Have more than one source of income at a time.
37. Read two books a month.
38. Buy a Chanel bag because they're always in style.
39. Live somewhere I can walk or drive to buy groceries.
40. World peace.

As I reviewed the list I wrote half a lifetime ago, a chill slid down my spine. Dazed, I realized my old goals were my current reality.

I lived the life I had described at twenty-two years old. I lived in a cozy Cape Cod home in the Chicago suburbs, a few miles from Lake Michigan. I had married my best friend, David, and we wanted to start a family. We adopted our dog, Watson, arguably the cutest pup ever. My sister and brother-in-law lived in Chicago, so we regularly went together to museums and restaurants and listened to live music. For more than a decade, I had worked in health care communications—a field that constantly changed and provided new challenges. I traveled. I had mastered the beachy wave with my straightening iron.

I fit into the perfect paradigm of a white, middle-class, almost middle-aged professional married woman. Check, check, check.

I only had one problem: I'd never been more miserable in my life.

Yes, I know how ungrateful and privileged I sound. Like any respectable Catholic woman, I'm well-acquainted with guilt. I felt fortunate and grateful for everything I had. Yet beneath that veneer of Instagram-worthy moments, my carefully curated world was falling apart, and no amount of willpower could fix it. Typically, I could fix things with sheer force. Not this time. This was adult life. Real life. I was not in control.

It was all big stuff. My husband was grieving the passing of his mother. We had a miscarriage and unexplained infertility. We underwent IVF treatments for two years—a roller coaster of joy and despair. More grief. I learned my parents were ill. I could not help; we were separated due to the pandemic. Work was a mess. I was lost in corporate politics; I had no hope of regaining my footing. Work no longer provided a source of comfort.

I had failed in every way: as a wife, a daughter, a professional, and a woman.

I couldn't wake up in the morning because I was depressed. Yet, in a cold sweat, I'd jolt awake in the middle of the night and grab my husband's hand until he told me to go back to sleep. My weight fluctuated. I numbed my body's sensations with caffeine, alcohol, and food to keep working, performing, and climbing. I disengaged from my body and its sensations with the added IVF hormones and recent traumatic events. I no longer recognized myself in the mirror.

So, like any respectable wellness junkie, my first reaction was to find other people who could tell me what to do. Some might call me a seeker. Some might call me a privileged woman with too much time on her hands. I'm not afraid to look for healing and direction in various places.

I tried it all:

- Retreats at convents where I sang psalms with nuns
- Shamans spat on my neck to close snakebites from another lifetime
- Too many tarot and psychic readings to count
- Sound and water baths
- Astrological workshops
- Jungian, cognitive behavioral, and retail therapy
- Pharmaceutical assistance
- The occasional crystal

This time, things were different. I was not well. This wasn't a matter of recovering from a disappointing date or a bad week at the office. My general health and closest relationships were suffering. I needed a different approach and a solution that would have a lasting impact—not a fleeting sensation I would chase again and again.

That's when I made a critical realization. I lost sight of myself.

I was attempting to fit myself into an idealized version of who I thought I *should be* instead of who *I was*. For years, I dutifully followed a list I created at twenty-two, but that list didn't leave room for life's messiness, the occasional mistake, or fun.

So I dug deeper. I asked myself some difficult questions.

Is this the life I want? Or is it the life I think I should have?

Who is that sad-looking woman in the mirror? When was the last time she felt and looked happy? Why isn't she doing things that make her happy?

How many days in succession have I worn these yoga pants, and when was the last time I did yoga?

Is that gray hair in my eyebrow?

I also followed a pattern of putting myself into situations I did not enjoy to fit into the "successful" category. Those situations often went sideways and ended with an embarrassing moment I would relive for years afterward.

I learned the cost of fitting in is too high. I needed to embrace what made me different—what made me, me. It sounds easy. However, I spent years ignoring my instincts in search of what I thought I should do, have, or want.

So if you feel lonely or different, I've been there. Maybe you never fit in or briefly lost your way. Consider me a temporary guide, and I'll show you how I reconnected with my personal brand of weirdness, with what made me happy.

How? You'll see. But I promise you this: when I embraced my differences and stopped trying to fit in, I ended up where I belonged.

1.

LEFT, LEFT, LEFT WHEN OTHERS ARE RIGHT

EXIT STAGE LEFT
I was a theater kid who never acted, sang, or danced.

This tiny technicality did not sway me. I identified as a theater kid. My heart belonged to the stage. The fame and fortune that comes with a life devoted to the theater arts would sweep me away in only a matter of time. This passion. This devotion. This *je ne sais quoi*. All the world was a stage, my friends, and who were we but performers?

Who are we, indeed? In the 1980s Ozarks, I can tell you what we weren't: regular attendees at the Met or Guggenheim. In Springfield, Missouri, the art scene was scant, and my father, an art professor in our town, was at the center of that scarcity. Cue the sad violin.

My parents were determined to expose us to the art education they could access. Every vacation included a museum trip in which I'd take in halls of art with wide eyes. I spent hours sitting on a wooden step in my dad's art studio, watching him paint. My mom always played classical music in our house and introduced me to the theater. Despite that, we were not a family of intellectuals waxing poetic in the Ozark hills. It wasn't all highbrow. Oh, no.

My kryptonite was musicals. A magical movie or play with costumes, a string of "numbers," and loosely formed plots where the guy gets the gal and no one knows why or how, and it doesn't matter. All that matters is their toes tapped, perfectly in sync, and their voices soared. Why talk when you could sing?

I forced this love of musicals upon others. My younger sister, Sarah, was the unfortunate recipient of an unofficial musical theater curriculum. Almost six years my junior, I cajoled her into watching *The Sound of Music*, *The Wizard of Oz*, *My Fair Lady*, *White Christmas*, and *Hello, Dolly!* on repeat. I begged her to sing alto parts whenever there was a duet, and "tap dance" with me on tile floors while wearing our new patent leather shoes that we were supposed to wear on Easter Sunday.

IT'S SHOWTIME
At ten years old, musical film studies and lip-synching were no longer enough to satisfy my love for the theater arts. It was time to take this to the next level. I sang in the church choir, occasionally cantered, and was told I had a "nice voice." Later, I was told, "It wasn't a theater voice

but a choral voice. You know, one that is pretty when it blends in with other voices around it." Subtle feedback.

"You have a pretty soprano," the choir leader said.

"Thank you! I think I'd like to try out for the school play," I said.

My choir leader smiled and tilted her head. "It's such a nice choral voice."

Okay, so choir wasn't my path to stardom.

I had a comprehensive knowledge of musicals. Why postpone my destiny? I would fit in with that ragtag world of performers. I was destined to play a part in it.

Our community theater was hosting an open casting call for *Annie*. This was my chance. I was going to audition for the role of an orphan. Why not go for the starring role?

Because, as I found out, one must be strategic in show business. Don't be greedy. Manage expectations. Get your foot in the door before you start climbing the ladder.

I even went to a real voice coach for one hour to prepare for the role. The lesson cost twenty-six dollars, a sacrifice for my parents. I made use of the time. We chose a song for my audition that was within my range and kept me from going too far into my "head voice" and transitioning in and out of uncomfortable octaves. I was to sing "Honey

Bun" from *South Pacific*. Voice Coach suggested something a little *vaudeville*—whatever that meant.

I was ready to stun the directors at my audition. My ten-year-old self was prepared to sing a "vaudevillian" song. The song was about a young woman called "Honey Bun," sung by a slightly older woman pretending to be a man. Very Shakespearian. So many layers.

One week before the audition, the phone rang. Mom answered.

"Who was that?" I asked when she hung the heavy receiver back on its cradle.

"Your voice teacher," my mom said carefully.

I paused and put down my punctured Capri Sun bag.

"Oh. Voice Coach?" It had become my habit to call her thus.

My mom lifted an eyebrow. "Yes. Voice Coach. She said so many girls are auditioning for *Annie* that the directors are changing the audition format."

My heart squeezed, and palms sweat. "How is it changing? How many girls are *so many*?"

"They're asking all the girls to sing 'Tomorrow' instead of a prepared song."

"What about 'Honey Bun'? And vaudeville?"

"I'm sorry." Mom was sympathetic.

I slumped onto a swivel stool and pushed away my Capri Sun.

"But you know 'Tomorrow' already. You sing it all the time."

I considered this. "I do. I know all the words." I tapped my fingers against my chin. Should I see Voice Coach again? No. Another twenty-six dollars was out of the question.

"There's more, hon," Mom said. "Auditions will . . . well, they won't be individual."

"What does that mean?"

"They'll put you in groups to see how you perform together. And you'll need to dance."

"Will they show me what to do?" I did not have a Dance Coach.

"Yes. Someone will show you the steps and you will repeat them."

I briefly thought of tap dancing while wearing my patent leather shoes. "Okay. I wish you could be there, Mom." *Because this will be the day my life changes forever.*

My parents would be out of town. Our neighbor, Vicky, would be watching my sister and me. I loved Vicky, but shouldn't my mom and dad be there for this monumental occasion?

I decided the audition adjustment was fine. I knew every line to *Annie*—the Broadway and movie versions. I didn't dance, but how hard could it be? I already had a leg up on these other girls, didn't I? I had a wealth of knowledge about musicals and the most crucial thing. Heart.

STAGE MOMS

Now to choose an outfit. I looked at my closet, and everything seemed worn and sad—nothing that said "confident" or "pulled together" for being onstage. The glittery puff, paint-swirl T-shirt I made at the mall was inappropriate for the theater—even if it was a daytime audition. I would not wear formal The Eagles Eye dresses or holiday sweaters my grandmother sent me from Philadelphia. While they were all "good quality" and "preppy" and "what everyone wore on the Main Line," they did not translate to Springfield, Missouri, on a Saturday afternoon.

No. I needed a pulled-together baby biz casual look that could be dressed up or down. I needed the equivalent of a little black dress for up-and-coming ten-year-olds trying to make an impression. I needed a look that said, "I'm confident but not cocky. I'm put together but not trying too hard. I'm quirky but not weird. I'm ready to sing and dance and act because I am a theater kid, and I am home." *Bingo!* I had it: one of my father's too-big button-down shirts with the sleeves rolled up and worn "bloused out," tight-rolled black jeans, and my high-top black Reebok sneakers with two Velcro straps—because I would be dancing after all. Hair? A side ponytail to keep things *fresh*.

When it was time to leave, my five-year-old sister saw me in my sweet ensemble.

"Is that Daddy's shirt?" Sarah eyed me suspiciously. In her way, Sarah asked a perfectly reasonable question, but it had a sisterly subtext I understood.

"Yes," I looked down at my outfit and back into her calm face.

"Oh," she said.

I knew she meant, "I don't have the vocabulary to express this yet, but I'm concerned. Today is a big day for you. I know you have a lot of emotional stock riding on this experience, but I think you're starting to spiral. Let's take this outfit. Why in the world did you decide to wear one of Dad's shirts? We don't even know if it's been properly cleaned, it doesn't fit, and here you are trying to Scarlett O'Hara yourself into some sort of costume. Do your delusions of grandeur have no limits? I'll go along with this and support you because I love you, but please know I have reservations."

We both knew I was a lost cause.

* * *

The interior of our community theater was truly the most beautiful place in the world. The Springfield Landers Theater was always magical, decorated with gold paint and pink velvet. Faux Rococo ceilings, tiny seats, narrow stairways to the balcony, and carved faces in the building's façade. It was the most beautiful landmark in our city, and I wanted so badly to be part of its magic.

My transition from the lobby to the stage is blurry. I recall climbing onto the grand stage and standing in a row with nine other girls. Then, certain details become crystal clear and will be locked in every lobe of my brain for the rest of my life.

The expansive stage, adorned with thick red velvet curtains and golden tassels, reached opposite ends of the earth. The domed ceiling crowned the theater with pastel and golden flowers and cherubs. In reality, it was a relatively small but well-maintained community theater. In my eyes, I stood beneath the great dome of St. Paul's Cathedral in London.

A woman with thick glasses interrupted my revelry and gave me a large paper square printed with the number eight. I pinned it to my father's shirt. I hoped the pin didn't leave noticeable holes so my dad wouldn't get mad when he returned.

I found my place in the line of girls. I smiled politely at them, but the smile never reached my eyes. I looked into the audience, but the white stage lights blinded me.

Onstage, I floated above the earth, and it was terrifying and thrilling.

"Young ladies! I am pleased so many pretty little girls are here to try out for this play." An enthusiastic, thin, middle-aged man with glasses clapped his hands and spoke to everyone in the auditorium. "Remember, we're all here to have fun and do our best," he noted, looking over his wire-framed lenses with a knowing smile.

From the balcony, a few mothers dressed in fluorescent windbreakers clapped enthusiastically in response. A large number of people sat in the audience.

Who let all of them in here?

I was supposed to audition before the casting director and other professionals. Not this motley crew of pushy parents and...

Oh no, Sarah and Vicky are watching too? Why do all the moms already know the thin, middle-aged man in charge?

Small-town community theater politics never crossed my mind before the audition, but many people already had an in.

I looked down the line of girls next to me and assessed the competition. A couple girls looked pale and like they might pass out. Most were closer to seven or eight years old. I panicked. Had I already aged out of the orphan demographic? A washed-up actress at age ten. Then, I found one that might be twelve; it looked like she was developing already. One, likely six or seven years old, had freckles drawn on her face and wore giant ringlets in her hair. Her mother had dressed her like an insane Raggedy Ann doll in some psychological ninja move to suggest to the director she was already one of the orphans. Most girls wore pink, purple, and turquoise dresses with leggings and giant bows in their hair. They definitely didn't wear their father's button-downs and dark denim.

The piano began to play the introduction to "Tomorrow." I was third in line, so I wouldn't have to wait long before my turn. But these bastards didn't start at the beginning of "Tomorrow." No. They started at the song's primary crescendo like a bunch of sadists. The twelve-year-old beside me squeaked out something inaudible, and I lamented what it must be like to have boobs and fail so miserably. Tragic.

My turn came. I was aware of the introductory chords. I was also suddenly aware my voice could not, in any way, fill that theater. I sang something like "Tomorrow." A distinct difference fell into my voice when I had to change keys, which wasn't a good thing. I knew I was better than the girl next to me.

I also knew I wasn't good enough to be an orphan.

When I was finished, I squinted into the audience and saw my little sister wrapped in her purple winter coat with rosy cheeks, looking up at me with even, dead eyes.

I didn't blame her. This couldn't be fun for her, either. Vicky smiled politely, blandly.

Then, it was raging Raggedy Ann's turn. She didn't sing. She screamed. Her mom, wearing a fur coat with voluminous hair Christie Brinkley would be jealous of, was also screaming. "I cain't hear you, sweetheart! Louder, baby! Mama cain't hear you!"

My five-year-old sister and I shared a look. *Holy shit. What was that?* our eyes said.

As we neared the end of the line, I prepared to leave the stage, thoroughly defeated. Then it hit me. We were only halfway through the audition.

"Girls, get into two lines for the dance part of the audition," someone announced. I felt sick.

A woman, about twenty years old, arrived in a leotard, oversized sweatshirt, and some sort of soft dance shoe that was neither for ballet nor tap.

"Dancers! I'm Shanna, and I'll be doing the choreography for the final cast of *Annie*." She spoke animatedly. In fact, she never stopped moving and shimmied around onstage.

"I will show you a few step combinations and want you to repeat them. Now, watch me closely."

Shanna kicked off her leg warmers and sweatshirt and tossed them to the side. I was in way over my head, and now all I could do was follow directions as closely as possible, get out of this theater, and not return until we saw *The Nutcracker* at Christmas.

Shanna showed us a series of seemingly reasonable steps. Okay. Yes. Sure. I could replicate this. It had some sort of skip. Or was it a gallop? Left, left, left, right, right, right. That was the skip. Got it. No sweat. Windmill left. Windmill right. Jazz hands to the sky.

I had to admit; the sequence was inspired.

I heard, "Five, six, seven, eight," just like they said on *A Chorus Line*. Then, it was time to move. I sprang into action. At the same time, my mind went completely blank—a sheer kinetic force without direction or destination. I saw the other girls skipping and immediately started to skip.

Left, left, left, left, left, left.

I skipped in a half-moon shape in the opposite direction from the rest of the girls. Instead of going right after the third "left," I continued left. Quickly, I windmilled, reached to the sky with jazz hands, and completed my sequence . . . on the opposite side of the stage. The distance between the girls and me was five feet, but as far as I was concerned, the chasm between us was in a different hemisphere where people spoke a foreign language, and their winters were my summers.

I went left. The others were right. Sometimes, you need a physical stage that feels like the Grand Canyon to convince you that you can be passionate about something without making it your identity. My *Annie* audition was not my first misguided attempt to fit in, and it would not be my last.

I still love watching musicals, but I don't perform in them. More than thirty-five years after she watched me fail at my *Annie* audition, my sister, Sarah, invited me to watch *Hello Dolly!* at an old refurbished movie theater in downtown Chicago. Audience members could sing along. We were among them.

2.
PHYSICAL EDUCATION

THE GALLOWS

I blame President Eisenhower for my complicated relationship with exercise.

Apparently, President Eisenhower freaked out in post–World War II America when European children surpassed American children in physical fitness challenges (Boyle 1955). What was it about athletic Swiss kids that brought out President Eisenhower's competitive streak? I don't know.

I do know that instead of encouraging winter sports and an après-ski moment, President Eisenhower developed a President's Council of Youth Fitness and a pilot study called the Presidential Fitness Challenge. The challenge eventually became the Presidential Fitness Test, which did not resemble the original physical fitness challenges the American and Swiss children performed. Instead of focusing on core strength and flexibility, the test resembled a military training exercise and stayed in that format for decades (Edwards 2015).

The Presidential Fitness Test was the source of my physical fitness-related trauma.

Someone in the government decided US public school students needed to begin practicing for what would soon become the TV phenomenon *Ninja Warrior*. After a year of playing sharks and minnows and four square in PE class, we began military-grade trading. This training included the bent-arm hang, pull-ups, sit and reach, mile run, fifty-yard dash, and other crucial maneuvers in case we needed to escape a foxhole between the playground and a suburban housing development.

Like the Olympic Summer Games, Presidential Fitness Test season contained moments of triumph and despair.

My best event was sit and reach. It involved sitting. And reaching. I sat with my sneakers flush against the side of a dingy plastic milk crate and leaned forward. Wherever my tiny hobbit fingertips touched, that measurement indicated my flexibility. I always received an *E* at sit and reach. The *E* was for "Excellent" or "Exceptional." It could have been "Eh," but I don't think that's accurate.

My worst event was pull-ups. Pull-up day was inevitable, but I never acclimated to it. Pull-up day and I had a long-standing feud. We met every year, and it was always the same. Pull-up day included unnecessary rituals, questions, lies, disappointment, and humiliation. Oh yes. I knew pull-up day well. She was a cruel mistress, and she was consistent. Every year on pull-up day, I left the pull-up bars with the same score: zero.

When I was nine years old, I left our lunchroom with a sinking feeling in the pit of my stomach. No, it wasn't from my peanut butter and jelly sandwich and Juicy Juice drink combo. I knew in a few minutes, Elementary School Coach would lead me into the late May sunshine for the pull-up test. Since I ate PB&Js and skipped arm days at the gym, I also guessed my score.

After lunch, my classmates and I followed Elementary School Coach outside onto the hot playground. I felt like I was in an old Western movie, standing in the dust and sun with a sense of dread.

It was almost high noon—pull-up time.

Three metal pull-up bars of various heights stood on the left side of a concrete path. The bars baked in the relentless Missouri sun all morning and gleamed in the white heat. Elementary School Coach placed three semi-sturdy plastic milk crates under each pull-up bar. She then divided us into separate lines—one per pull-up bar.

"All right, everyone! I want to see three single-file lines facing the bars," she announced and pointed to the bars. "Matt, Jennifer, and Lindsey, you're up first."

My classmates and I shuffled into our lines to watch the scene unfold. The chosen ones climbed the milk crates to those scorching metal bars.

"Is everyone ready?" Elementary School Coach prepared for their demise.

Jennifer and Lindsey stared ahead at the cloudless sky, refusing to look at her. Matt gave her a sideways glance and nodded, indicating he was ready for what would come next.

One by one, she kicked the plastic milk crates from under their feet, and the children were left to either hang miserably in the spring breeze or fight the good fight and lift themselves to the bar.

Immediately, Lindsey fell to the ground. Her white, limp arms gave out, and she had no interest in making this moment last longer than necessary. Jennifer fought her way to the top of that bar, and by God, her chin touched it.

"One!" Elementary School Coach counted and captured it on her clipboard. Jennifer struggled, trying to reach the bar again, but it was no use. She eased off the pull-up bar and knew it was a noble performance.

Matt, the final boy, was a short, fast, and muscular soccer player. He seemed physically incapable of sitting in his seat during class. At this moment, he repeatedly lifted himself to the bar like some mechanized toy. His friends counted aloud for him and cheered him on. He reached five, then eight, then ten. At eleven, he jumped down, brushed off his hands good-naturedly, and smoothed his hair. He wasn't even out of breath.

I was, naturally, after him in line.

"Next group!"

I stepped forward with two classmates, each representing one of the three lines, simultaneously accepting our fate. I walked toward the scorching pull-up bar and stood before my classmates. I looked into their eyes, and they looked into mine. Some eyes held pity and understanding because they knew my fate. They knew how this event would end for me. I saw judgment and scorn in others' eyes as though they knew I had no strength or endurance for this feat. No matter.

Let them watch. I looked away bitterly.

"Step onto the crates!" Elementary School Coach ordered.

With tentative feet, I climbed onto the wobbly red plastic crate. It shook beneath me, and I tried to reclaim my balance and what was left of my dignity. The line of children in front of me stopped momentarily and held their breath, anticipating a fall. When I regained my composure, they spoke out of the sides of their mouths as they watched and waited for the beginning of the end.

"Hands on the bars!"

I lifted my arms and wrapped my fingers around the pull-up bar. I looked beyond my classmates and focused on the surrounding landscape. It was one of those hot days when the heat above asphalt made the air shift and move. On the playground, beneath each swing, the earth eroded and the dust and dirt flew in the wind.

A hawk circled in the sky, searching for easy prey. The world could be cruel to an eight-year-old girl participating in Presidential Fitness Tests, but I could also appreciate its stark beauty.

I briefly looked to my right at the classmates who joined me in my fate. Mandy looked back at me and smiled weakly. I smiled back—a shared understanding and sense of compassion. Julie stared at the ground, lost in her thoughts.

"Ready?" asked the Elementary School Coach.

We replied in unison.

"Ready."

"Whatever."

"Not really."

Then, Elementary School Coach walked behind us one by one and kicked the crate from under our legs. I jolted when she kicked my crate. She watched my attempt to regain my footing. I held on to the hot bar and felt gravity urge me back to the safe and solid ground.

I negotiated with my body in what took several seconds but felt like a millennium. I checked in with my arm muscles, back, and stubby fingers.

Arms, I thought. *I know we've never completed a pull-up before, but what if this year is different? What if we show everyone standing in that line that we can do this? Kids do it all the time. We can't be that different.*

I paused and gave my arms a moment to respond.

No way, my lifeless arms replied.

Traitors.

What about you, back and shoulder muscles?

We barely connect your arms to the rest of your body. You're lucky we showed up today, they said.

Hands and fingers?

You're losing your grip on that pull-up bar and *reality,* my hands and fingers huffed.

What else here could make this happen? I swear I'll go outside more. I plea-bargained with my own body.

The answer was no. My body was useless and unresponsive.

Beads of sweat ran down my back, and I desperately wanted to visit the water fountain. I wanted to return to my cool classroom with bright-colored calendars highlighting people's birthdays. I wanted soothing images of how to write the alphabet in cursive. Why did I have to bake outside in this inferno and pretend to suddenly have physical capabilities we all knew I didn't have? It was a farce. It was embarrassing for everyone involved.

Okay, then. I decided.

Oh, she's really going to do it? my body whispered.

Why delay the inevitable?

I blissfully released the bar and dropped onto solid ground. Then, I politely moved the milk crate under the bar for the next victim and left my place at the gallows. I checked my hands for blisters and injuries because I had a piano lesson later that day and didn't want to look garish.

"Zero, Mora?" asked Elementary School Coach with one raised eyebrow.

"At least I kept my record." I spoke over my shoulder, focused on making my way to the water fountain. Then, I turned to look at the pull-up bar, burning in the unforgiving heat.

See you next year, compadre. We would meet again one year later, whether I wanted to or not.

As if on cue, the hawk flew away to search for prey in another field.

JERSEY GIRL

Athletic humiliation was not relegated to land. The school system could also apply it to water as well.

"As you all know, your swimming module begins next week," Elementary School Coach told my fifth-grade class. Every year, Springfield Public Schools shuttled nine-year-olds to the local YMCA for an off-site swimming module.

Yes! I squeezed my hands together in excitement.

"Remember your signed approval forms," Elementary School Coach noted.

Got it. I wrote a reminder in blue ink on the back of my hand and made a mental note.

"Don't forget to dress comfortably that day." She turned on her heels and led us out of the gym.

Why would that matter? We're wearing our bathing suits.

I was too excited to dwell on details. This was a guaranteed daily field trip for a week, and I could swim. I could not hit, kick, bounce, or throw a ball, but I could glide through the water. While I grew up in a land-locked state, I knew my way around a dog paddle, backstroke, and butterfly.

My family and I visited my grandparents' home on Long Beach Island, New Jersey, every summer. It sat neatly between a bay and the ocean, so we regularly spent days at the beach. I preferred to spend as much time as possible in the sea, underwater, or on a boogie board, coasting on waves toward the shore.

On Long Beach Island, my family ate dinners on the back porch. I drank whole cans of Diet Coke and enjoyed freshly steamed crabs, scallops, and mussels while my parents sipped on gin and tonics. Frank Sinatra crooned in the background until dishes were cleared and we fell into bed, exhausted from long days in the sun and salt water.

I soon learned the Springfield Public Schools swimming module would not be a summer at the shore. Instead, it would warp an activity I loved into something twisted and unnatural.

* * *

I boarded an old yellow school bus for the local YMCA on swim module day. Everyone gossiped about what they heard about the swim classes from the sixth graders and their older brothers and sisters.

"We have to change in the locker room. Into bathing suits," said Jennifer.

Will we see each other naked? My heart stopped, and I sat in stony silence. My family was modest. I never went to summer camp, played sports, or changed in front of teammates.

"I heard they divide us into groups based on a swimming test," Lindsey, my seatmate, bit her nail.

I'm not the worst swimmer. Lindsey still won't go into the deep end. I tucked this piece of information into the back of my head and assessed my classmates. I hoped I wasn't the worst swimmer since I swam often, but I didn't know others' experience levels.

Will I be tested? Will I tread water? Dog paddle? Hold my breath underwater?

I had so many unanswered questions.

* * *

At the ancient yellow-brick-covered Y, my classmates and I filtered out of the bus and into the old building. The dim foyer echoed with faint whistles and carried the sharp smell of chlorine. A volunteer ushered us into the boys' and girls' locker rooms to dress for the module.

In that locker room, I was no longer a mermaid or surfer on the Jersey shore. I was a cautionary tale in a 1950s public service announcement.

First, we received our new swimming gear. A stocky woman with fluffy blonde hair held up our "uniform." Everyone in the room either inhaled sharply or stopped breathing. The swimsuit was nothing like the '80s swimsuits we knew and loved. The suit did not have pink, purple, or turquoise bows and ruffles. No edgily placed neon racing stripes. Instead, they were high-necked swimsuits in primary colors. Their legs cut straight across the top of our thighs, similar to styles from the 1950s and 1960s.

To accessorize the suits, the stocky woman offered old white plastic swimming caps complete with chin straps to protect our hair from the dangers of chlorinated water. I never dreamed I would wear something so stupid. Yet this woman dangled it before me between her pearly polished thumb and forefinger.

"Which color do we wear?" Jennifer asked bravely while others tried to regain consciousness.

Who cared? The color was the least of our issues. I wasn't worried whether the swimsuit hue would bring out the color of my eyes. *Look at that cut! And those stupid caps!* No one mentioned the caps.

"You'll be given a color based on your size," the woman with dandelion fluff hair noted matter-of-factly.

Instantly, I cared about color. Girls eyed each other, assessing their size and which color they would be. I was definitely on the larger side of the size spectrum. A gracious friend once said I was big-boned, but I knew anatomy didn't work that way. It was unlikely that I had tree trunk bones while she had twigs.

Please don't let me be her size. I guiltily looked at certain girls and prayed I didn't look like them. But in my heart of hearts, I knew I did. I knew we would get the same color swimming suit.

Dandelion Head looked at me, surveyed me from head to toe, and gave me what must have been the large or extra-large swimsuit size. The green swimsuit was designated for the curvier fifth graders who carried extra weight or had begun developing breasts. Not that it accommodated a newly developed body with a bra or a specific shape. It was just big and green.

I looked around at the other green girls. Yeah—we knew who we were. Some of us were a little too into pudding snacks. Some of us had ethnic backgrounds that didn't fit the norm in this region. We were resigned and hoped to fade into the background with our newly provided green screens.

I opened a locker and attempted to hide behind it as I changed. I pulled my hair into a ponytail, stuffed it under the painful plastic cap that squeezed my skull, and pulled at the tiny hairs on either side of my face. I grabbed goggles and looked at myself in the mirror. It was awful. A chubby girl stuffed into a green bathing suit with a golf ball for a head.

Could this get any worse?

Oh yes, it could. As I turned the corner, I realized what my petite classmates were forced to wear. The tiniest ladies in my class wore pale yellow bathing suits that left little to the imagination. What happened when we got into the pool? What pervert signed off on this dress code? We all stood in the locker room waiting for further directions, unable to meet one another's eyes.

"Okay, ladies! Let's hit the pool!" said Dandelion Head.

Nothing could have prepared us for what we were about to see. As we exited the locker room in synchronized swimming uniforms, we found our male classmates waiting. They stood in a line, trying to cover themselves, wearing tiny black form-fitting bathing suits. We were more accustomed to a swim trunk cut, but my mom described this style as "European." I immediately forgot about my swimming cap.

In short, nothing says *humiliating* like a bathing suit sanctioned by the State of Missouri whose state slogan is, ironically, the "Show Me State."

* * *

The swimming instructors assessed our skills in the pool. We dog-paddled, floated on our backs, and attempted a backstroke. At the end of the exercises, the instructors divided us into three groups: one, two, and three. I was placed into group three, a smaller group with only boys so far. Immediately, I was self-conscious in my green swim ensemble and missed my girlfriends. At least we could gossip and commiserate together.

Walking away from my friends toward the pool's deep end with group three, I looked longingly at Lindsey in group two.

How will I cope with dudes in Speedos? I pleaded with my eyes. Where would I look?

She gave me an encouraging smile as I followed YMCA Coach to the pool's deep end. YMCA Coach then demonstrated a backstroke and told us to swim across the length of the deep end and back.

Okay. I can do this. Just follow the lines on the ceiling, and don't drift too far to the right or left. I stood nervously in line behind two guys who playfully punched each other and pretended to throw one another in the pool. I kept my distance to avoid being hit.

When it was my turn, I jumped into the pool and kicked off against the wall. I loved the cool, smooth sensation when swimming. Underwater, the quiet, otherworldly sounds were always peaceful. I eased into a rhythm and floated through the water.

I noticed one of the boys smirking at me out of the corner of my eye. I panicked and stopped my meditative movement.

What was so funny? Was I off course?

I checked my surroundings but was still swimming in a straight line. I checked my nose and face to see if something was on it. No, nothing. I felt exposed, and the pool was no longer safe and soothing. I imagined what they saw—a chubby girl in a green swimsuit and swim cap floating around on her back like a helpless sea turtle.

"Keep going!" urged YMCA Coach.

I snapped to attention. I looked away from the boys and returned to my backstroke. Then, my mind processed another narrative.

Group three included the boys who were on swim teams last summer. This must have been the advanced swimming group. So I must have been a good swimmer too. *I am the only girl here, but I am good enough to be here.*

I loved swimming and being in the water. My mom always called me her "little fish," and it made me flush with pride. Swimming made me happy and reminded me of being in beautiful places with my family and feeling strong and independent. How dare this dumb class and stupid boys make me feel bad?

On Long Beach Island, New Jersey, people said wise things like "fuggedaboutit" or "that guy can kiss my ass" (my Pop Pop frequently used this phrase). So I decided to *fuggedabout* them. I turned my head toward the ceiling and swam with newfound confidence. I was the girl in group three, and the boys needed to get used to the idea.

As the swimming module wore on, I didn't worry about my ridiculous outfit. Sometimes I won swimming relays and races. I felt stronger and started to have fun again.

One day, a class bully almost ruined the fun. He made a comment about my green swimsuit and its size. I looked down at his Speedo.

"It's probably good the guys' suits aren't color-coordinated, huh? Yours would be really small."

Did I really know what I was talking about? No. But I knew enough to land an insult. At that moment, I also won the respect of every boy in group three.

* * *

I learned an important lesson in my swimming module unrelated to the backstroke or butterfly: If you're at your most vulnerable, remember what makes you happy and keep going.

Also, if you can access her, find your inner Jersey girl. Summon that siren from the depth of your being. She will arise within you, tell everyone to kiss your ass, and make a snide comment about the size of some guy's shorts. She will awaken strength within you and usher you to your proverbial Jersey shore.

3.

LITTLE MEN

I feel a kinship with Candice Bergen.

Not for portraying a feisty broadcast journalist in her Emmy- and Golden Globe-winning role in the *Murphy Brown* sitcom, modeling on the cover of *Vogue*, or choosing to become a single mother in the face of criticism. I feel connected to her because she accomplished these things despite being raised in a home with ventriloquist dummies. Candice Bergen gave me hope.

Dad's ventriloquism hobby started innocently enough. He grew up watching the *Howdy Doody* show and listening to Edgar Bergen and his dummy, Charlie McCarthy, on the *Edgar Bergen and Charlie McCarthy* radio show. They were wise-cracking, silly, and funny characters who said things most people never could. I'm sure this appealed to my reserved dad and gave him an excuse to act out and say what he thought. Pardon the pop psychology.

When he was eight years old, my grandfather gave Dad a ventriloquist dummy named Jerry Mahoney. My dad loved his dummy and practiced speaking without moving his lips and could spar just like old Edgar did with Charlie on their show. Somewhere hidden in a dusty trunk, Dad still has a black-and-white photograph of himself as a young boy, dressed in a dapper suit, performing with Jerry at a school talent show. You could tell my dad was taking this seriously, and—I wager because he's a perfectionist—he was the best junior ventriloquist in Moorhead, Minnesota.

When I came on the scene, my dad pursued ventriloquism as a hobby. He only performed in front of close friends who showed an appreciation for ventriloquism or after having one to two highballs. Typically, audience members included my parents' elderly friends who remembered the 1940s and 1950s or my eccentric high school friends who begged my dad to perform. My dad was more interested in the craftsmanship and mechanics of the ventriloquist dummies and not in performing.

He collected and created ventriloquist dummies by carving them from basswood or developing elaborate molds for their faces. The dummies also had names and back stories inspired by his childhood. Many characters hailed from northern Minnesota and North Dakota, similar to those from NPR's "The News from Lake Wobegon."

"Arnie Softing was one of the Softing boys that lived up der on de farm." My dad started stories in a *Fargo* accent.

He paired these subtle characters with wildly expressive faces and eyes constantly shifting from side to side. The eyes arrived in boxes from local taxidermists.

For my dad, an artist, dummies represented a form of imagination, play, and whimsy. For my sister and me, they were just really, really weird.

Dad displayed six dummies he collected throughout adulthood—Russell, Jerry Mahoney, two Charlie McCarthys—a big one and a small one, and Will E. Talk—in our living room on top of a large armoire where they watched us. The dummies' faces expressed they were on the precipice of saying something.

Help us, won't you? their eyes asked. *We're stuck on this armoire and cannot get down!*

I avoided their gazes. Their constant presence was fertile ground for nightmares.

I read *The Velveteen Rabbit* and saw *The Nutcracker* and knew that, at night, when everyone was asleep, the dummies came alive, roamed our house, listened to our music, plotted murders, ate snacks, or whatever else ventriloquist dummies did for fun. Specifically, I imagined them going through our cupboards at 2:00 a.m. and stealing my dad's favorite snacks like Ritz crackers, sharp cheddar cheese, summer sausage, and the occasional Corona beer.

I believed Russell—the most terrifying dummy—led the other dummies as a small army of wooden creepsters. His bright white face and red lips starkly contrasted against his eyes—black dots in the center of outlined circles. These eyes gave him a distant, zombie-like stare. He wore a black wig and plaid shirt and dungarees.

"He's a wonderful example of folk art," Mom explained seriously.

Okay. I guess I hate folk art. I still associate anything primitive and disturbing with "folk art."

The other dummies wore more formal attire—suit jackets, top hats, and saddle shoes or oxfords. While also disturbing, at least these guys made an effort with their appearance.

Like most things we live with, I occasionally forgot about the dummies and their lifelike presence. Sometimes, they blended into my parents' eclectic home decorations, including art, textiles, and books, and were as unobtrusive as a throw pillow.

All it took was one new friend's reaction to the dummies to remind me they were not normal decor. I could not treat them like my grandmother's cross-stitch sampler. There was nothing quite like inviting someone inside the house for a glass of lemonade and watching them come face-to-face with the dummy pack. The exchange typically went like this:

"What are those?"

"Oh yeah. Those. Well . . . they're my dad's ventriloquist dummies."

"What?"

"Yeah. He," I hedge, looking for an explanation, "liked *Howdy Doody* as a kid."

"Who is Howdy Doody?"

"He was a ventriloquist dummy from the 1950s. His character was a," I frown at my friend's blank face, "never mind."

"They're really freaky."

"I know."

"Can your dad talk without moving his mouth?"

"Yeah."

"That's kind of cool."

"I guess so."

"Don't they creep you out?"

"I'm used to them. But they still freak me out at night."

My friend nods in agreement. "That makes sense."

The dummies made slumber parties and sleepovers a hard sell at my house. When it came to choosing whether you wanted to hang at Jennifer's for a barbeque and time in the hot tub or head over to Mora's house for caffeine-free Diet Pepsi and a swarm of motionless wooden dolls smiling at you, I don't think the decision was tough for most people.

It's fine, ladies. Tuck yourselves into your sleeping bags while the little ventriloquist dummy men watch you sleep. If you hear something, don't open your eyes. It will only upset them.

As a tween, I knew plenty of kids who liked to stay up at night and watch horror movies, but I could not stomach them. Not surprisingly, I refused to watch the Chucky movies or anything where possessed dolls played a prominent role. Watching those characters neatly separated from you on a screen is one thing. Watching them while another doll sat in the same room with you was another.

What if I started giving the ventriloquist dummies violent ideas that had never occurred to them? Or what if I hurt their feelings because they were peaceful people who fought violent stigmas that late-eighties movies thrust upon them? Maybe the whole thing was more of a public relations and image issue. Either way, I was not prepared to take that on.

DON'T BE SUCH A DUMMY

One evening when I was eleven years old, I groggily woke up and looked at my digital alarm clock, which read 1:32 a.m. The tree branches outside my bedroom window created shadows that shifted and shimmered with every gust of wind. I tried ignoring the shadows. I also tried ignoring the awareness that I really needed to use the bathroom.

Why did I have that cup of water before bed? I cursed myself because now my bladder was full. Now I had to contend with my most irrational fear: crossing our hallway at nighttime while the dummies came alive and looked at me.

Our split-level home's stairway was in line with the old pine armoire. The dummies sat on top, and, according to my overactive imagination, they slowly turned their heads to watch me scamper across the hallway toward the bathroom in the middle of the night. Rationally—yes—I knew this was completely ridiculous. But at 1:00 a.m., when you are a kid in a dark house with ventriloquist dummies, the rational self is not in charge.

First, I tried burying myself under my rose-patterned comforter and going back to sleep, but my bladder was too powerful.

Don't think about it. Just go back to sleep. I tried counting backward from one hundred. I tried thinking about school. My attempts to distract myself didn't work. I really had to go, and the situation went from a green to a yellow alert.

I considered calling for my mom or dad, but that was a baby move, and I hadn't called for my parents in two years. No, I needed to handle this maturely. I needed to go to the bathroom in the middle of the night like a confident, grown-ass adult.

So, dressed in my Beauty and the Beast nightgown—like an adult—I quietly padded across the carpet toward my bedroom door and opened it with a slight creak. My parents' door was slightly ajar and my little sister's door was open too. Everything was quiet except for soft snoring and rustling branches outside.

This was my moment of truth. I needed to cross the hall before the dummies could hear and, ever so slightly, turn their heads and rest their dead eyes upon me.

When they looked at me, I was petrified. While I couldn't confirm how the magic worked, I knew I'd be so terrified I might as well turn to stone.

I closed my eyes, said a Hail Mary, held my breath, and ran across the hall to the bathroom. I blacked out during the sprint because I don't remember running. However, I arrived safely in the bathroom, used the facilities, washed my hands, and threw cold water on my face to calm down. But the trek was only half over. I still had to make the return journey to my room. I took a deep breath and tried to push away the haunting scenarios creeping into my consciousness.

First, they'd follow me with their eyes. My imagination ran wild. Then, they'd climb down the armoire and run up the stairs, giving chase. One would reach out a clunky wooden hand and grab my leg as I crossed the hall.

"No!" I yelled. In my bare feet, I raced back down the hall to my room, and upon crossing the threshold to my safe haven, I raised my eyes to the ceiling and stretched like an Olympic runner who completed her final race of the season.

I made it. I smiled with deep satisfaction, and my heart rate slowed. I was ready to climb under my comforter again and hide under the sheets with Rebecca, my favorite stuffed animal.

Behind me, a floorboard creaked. Silhouetted in my bedroom's doorway was a small figure with cropped hair, no more than four feet tall. A dim light from the hallway shone behind the shadow as it stood motionless and watched me.

In a rush of adrenaline, I jumped in a way that can only be described as a triple axel. Without preamble, I leaped into the air, spun around three times, and landed on my bed. My heart pumped, and I opened my mouth but couldn't scream. I stared at the shadowy figure in the doorway.

"*Ister*, you left the bathroom light on," said the exasperated figure, who was my sister. Apparently, I woke her up with my fifty-yard dash and left the bathroom light on. She was weary from my nighttime antics.

"Sorry, Sarah." I was still catching my breath and clinging to the covers. She noticed I didn't make any movements toward the bathroom.

"I'll turn it off," she offered. While Sarah was wary of the dummies, her narratives about how terrifying they were had not yet developed.

Oh, how lucky to be young and naive.

"Good night, Sarah. Thank you," I said and meant it.

"Good night, 'Ister." She yawned, tiptoed to the bathroom, turned off the light, and returned to her bedroom.

* * *

Candice Bergen once described growing up with the ventriloquist dummy Charlie McCarthy. "Let's get one thing straight: I don't want your pity. [. . .] While technically an only child, I was always known—as a kid, at least—as 'Charlie's sister.' Now I want your pity" (Vanity Fair 2016).

For years, Dad's little men seemed like an inevitable strike against me in a campaign to be normal. While I didn't realize it, his dummies showed me the value of individualism, play, imagination, and pursuing personal passions and interests—despite what others think.

Regardless, I still won't go into my parent's basement alone at night, where they now display his Charlie McCarthy dummy. Charlie may be watching me, waiting for the right moment to introduce himself or offer me a Ritz cracker.

4.
TEAM SPORTS

DAISY CHAINS

As kids hit puberty, adults decide it's a good idea to remove safe, stable T-ball stands and allow volatile kids to throw softballs and baseballs at each other willy-nilly.

The summer when I was ten, my parents urged me to "get out of the house." It was a sticky Missouri summer, and I agreed to stand in hot dust pits throughout July and learn how to play softball with some of my athletic friends. I was hesitant to leave my air-conditioned basement and VCR for a softball field, but I did want to see my buddies. So I agreed.

We practiced swinging, stealing bases, and running drills. We exercised as a team and drank orange Gatorade in the afternoon sun. We did not, however, learn the rules of softball. Unlike other kids on the team, I did not know the rules of baseball. We didn't watch it at home, and I didn't play it with friends. Sure, I knew I needed to hit the ball and run around the bases. Beyond that, things were unclear.

What's a shortstop? Why doesn't she just pick a base?

Should I run now? How about now? Now? No? What about . . . now? Oh, shoot.

Why would anyone purposefully fall when trying to run to a base? Doesn't that hurt?

That's probably why I played in the right outfield.

Our first softball game day was a scorcher. I saw my mom sitting on the metal bleacher seats. She fanned herself with a flier and drank McDonald's iced tea. I was so jealous. I detested feeling hot and sweaty and instantly felt grumpy and resentful. Not exactly the can-do attitude a coach wants to see at your first game.

I started the game in the outfield. No one could hit a ball beyond the bases, so I wasn't playing much. My attention span dwindled. To occupy myself, I counted the number of people in the stands. Then I sang songs from our school choir, the Disney Lyric Singers. I imagined myself in my blue Lyric Singers T-shirt with my name airbrushed on the back—so rad! One year, we performed a medley of songs from the 1950s and '60s. I sang these in the outfield, imagining every dance move and gesture we delivered while standing on rickety metal risers.

Somewhere in the distance, I heard a familiar voice yell my name. It broke through the edges of my choir performance, and panic set in.

Oh no. Softball Coach.

"Get the ball!" he yelled.

"What?" I pulled myself out of the daze and threw the daisy chain I had recently made back onto the ground.

"Go. Get. The ball!" he shouted, pointing to the softball rolling past my feet.

"Oh! Okay!" I said, waving my gloved hand.

I scrambled to the ground and tried to pick up the ball with my dad's old baseball glove. The glove was too big for me, but I didn't know they came in different sizes. I chased the ball, picked it up, and balanced it in the leather glove, assuming my job was done. I beamed and looked at my mom for encouragement.

"Throw it in!" yelled Softball Coach.

I stood still and looked at my options. I had no idea where to throw it.

"Okay!" I said agreeably.

So I just . . . threw it. I threw it to no one in particular. It was as though I hoped it would get to the person who needed it the most—like a bottled letter at sea, washing ashore.

My teammates looked at me, confused for a beat, but jumped into action and finished the play. One runner made it to first. They kept the second from making it to home base. I exhaled a sigh of relief and clapped at everyone's performance.

"Nice work, everyone," I said, emulating Softball Coach. My team side-eyed me and ran back to the bench. I tried to avoid singing, making daisy chains, and daydreaming for the rest of the game.

In hushed tones, Cristen, my best buddy and teammate, explained it would be better to catch the ball before it hit the ground. So if I saw it coming, I should run toward it. However, if it was closer to someone else, I could let them get it, which was more convenient. Cristen provided helpful input; nevertheless, I asked Jesus and Mary to keep the softball on the left side of the field for the rest of the day.

After the game, my mom inquired about my right outfield activities.

"So what were you doing out there?" She laughed.

"I was singing school choir songs and making a daisy chain." I sighed. My cheeks were hot from embarrassment and the summer sun.

She paused, noting my chagrin. We walked toward the car.

"Was it a good daisy chain?" she finally asked.

"Yeah. It was a pretty good one." I considered my craftsmanship.

"Well, that's good." She rubbed my back as I opened the passenger door.

That day, I realized I might not pitch or play first base that summer. It didn't matter. Mom reminded me she was on my team anyway.

TEAM G

In eighth grade, a trend raged through Cherokee Middle School like a wildfire that would not be stopped. Weirdly, it came in the form of tweens and teens trying out for the volleyball team. In 1992, some boys started wearing baggy jeans that showed Tommy Hilfiger boxer shorts. Girls tied flannel shirts around their midsection like belts. For some reason, the other hot new trend was playing volleyball.

I don't know what caused this craze, but the eight girls who dominated our sports teams suddenly contended with a hodgepodge of Gabrielle Reece wannabes. Band nerds, speech know-it-alls, and even the art class potheads came out of the woodwork.

Everyone wanted to get in the game—including me.

I had never participated in a team sport besides softball; however, Cherokee Middle School's coaches said anyone who wanted to play could play. I could try out for the varsity team—laugh!—and if I didn't make varsity, the coaches would place me on an additional team. Those teams would compete with other regional schools.

The best part? All players had their photographs taken and received a volleyball T-shirt. I suddenly loved the idea of giving my parents a picture of me with a trusted volleyball. I imagined them putting it in a large, gilded frame on mahogany desks.

"That's my Mora," they'd say to colleagues and friends. "Watch out for her spike!"

So I joined the ranks of young women who randomly needed to explore this sport. After all, I played in PE and vaguely understood the rules of the game.

My serve was good. My hand made contact with the ball, and it crossed the net a lot of the time. I ticked key volleyball skills off my fingers.

I couldn't spike yet, but I could set the ball. My teammates would do the heavy lifting from there. That was teamwork.

I was optimistic about the whole experience and saw it as a learning opportunity.

But first, I had to make it through tryouts.

I arrived at the gym with dozens of other girls. Every clique sent representatives to volleyball tryouts that day. The giant bows in their hair, dark goth makeup, and hemp necklaces identified them. Most shellacked their acne scars in Cover Girl foundation and doused themselves in Victoria's Secret Cucumber Melon body spray. It was the best and worst of tween reality in the early nineties.

Volleyball Coach demonstrated serving, setting, passing, and spiking skills. Then, she divided us into lines and threw volleyballs at us. We responded with a set, pass, or spike. After a few moves, we ran to the back of the line. We moved rapidly because the gym was packed with eager young athletes.

When it was my turn, Volleyball Coach tossed the ball, and I hit it. She flung one above my head, and I set it up. She threw another, and I knew it was intended for a spike. But my kinetic skills failed. Synapses shut down. I was frozen until the ball hit me square in the forehead.

Say something, you idiot!

"Uh, I'm okay!" I waved.

"Thanks," Volleyball Coach said without looking up at me and wrote something on her clipboard.

"Is that it?" I asked.

"That's it. Next."

Discouraged, I rubbed my forehead and walked toward the locker room. As I left, Assistant Volleyball Coach gave me a flier informing me I could pick up my official T-shirt next week and wear it for picture day. The volleyball coach would also announce my team on picture day, too.

Whoa. Next week, my life as a legitimate school athlete was about to begin. Everything would come together the following Thursday; however, I needed to remember my priorities.

Should I wear my hair up or down on photo day?

The following Thursday, I arrived at the gym early for my volleyball T-shirt, which was a proper nineties T-shirt.

Before the fashion industry regularly offered women's T-shirts, we wore heavy Hanes T-shirts cut for adult men or small boys. My beefy volleyball T-shirt was no exception. It was designed to fit a rectangular man with giant shoulders, arms three times the length of my own, and no discernable hips. The shirt was decorated with a gray-and-maroon Cherokee Native American headdress and flying volleyball graphics. The cultural appropriation versus celebration debate had not started in my hometown.

The cut suited a forty-year-old man, not a chubby, pubescent fourteen-year-old girl; however, this was not my first rodeo. In no time, I transformed the shapeless sack into something runway ready. I changed into my knock-off black nylon Umbro shorts in the girl's gym. I tucked in my new T-shirt and bloused it out. I rolled up my sleeves. I pushed down my socks. I spritzed my bangs with firm-hold hairspray. I swiped Clinique's bonus gift lipstick on my lips. Cover Girl compact powder covered all manner of sins. I checked my braces for traces of food. *Voila.* Picture-perfect.

Picture time came, and I stood in another line for ten minutes, waiting for my close-up. When it was my turn, the photographer told me to sit on the floor, bend one leg, lean on it, then drape my other arm over the volleyball.

No problem, buddy. Let's do this.

I kicked up my knee, leaned over that volleyball, put my arm around it, and smiled like we were best friends—laughing as old chums do. I looked into the lens and saw a flash. At last, I had my volleyball photo and wore a volleyball T-shirt. I was officially an athlete. Nothing could ruin my day.

Proud of my newfound athlete status, I thanked the photographer, crossed to a group of girls huddled around a corkboard outside the gym, and edged my way through the group.

Our varsity volleyball team comprised the same girls who dominated most of our school's sports. And rightfully so, I had to admit. They moved with ease and confidence I couldn't help but admire. They might annoy the shit out of me socially, but they were the best players.

Somehow, Volleyball Coach divided the remaining hundred girls into small volleyball teams.

I searched for my name. The teams were listed alphabetically.

A, B . . . okay. I scanned the list, searching for my name. *C, D . . . no, not there . . . E, F . . . G?*

That's right. I was on Team G.

Was there a team H? Thank God, there was a team H. Typically, school teams only consisted of a varsity, junior varsity, and maybe an A or B team, but I was definitely mid-alphabet.

I looked at my list of teammates and recognized some names. One had a severe back injury. One exclusively wore Keds to everything, including church and gym. One was a known nose picker.

These were the ladies with whom I would set and serve.

So be it.

The following week, I practiced after school for twenty minutes a day because each team needed time on the court. Naturally, Volleyball Coach prioritized the varsity team, so they received the most court time. Team G's turn to practice was a comedy of errors.

"You got it?"

"No."

"Ow!"

"Wait, I thought that was mine."

"Shoot. Sorry!"

"My bad!"

I was delusional in thinking this would be my breakout athlete moment. I thought I was a decent volleyball player when placed on a team with decent volleyball players. When placed with players of my caliber, I saw myself for who I was: a terrible volleyball player. I could not spike, and my set was shaky at best.

"Thompson! I'd like to see a little more hustle out there. You know, Ms. Martin goes for it much more than you," Volleyball Coach called during practice.

More than once, Volleyball Coach said my teammate with a severe back injury and back brace had more get-up-and-go than I did.

"Yeah. She's pretty hungry out there," I agreed, attempting athlete speak.

After twenty minutes of court time, I thanked the volleyball gods my exercise in humiliation had ended.

On our first game night, I sat with my fellow Team Gremlins—the affectionate new nickname for our team—and waited. The games started with varsity, and teams played in alphabetical order, so I knew we wouldn't play for a while.

At 4:00 p.m., players' parents, friends, and little brothers and sisters packed the bleachers to cheer on their favorites. The gym's fluorescent lights beamed on the team as they sent the volleyball over the net. As the hours passed, the hallways grew dim and the gym emptied. Team G slumped against a bleacher, drinking lukewarm Gatorade and Dr. Pepper. The excitement passed, and we were ready to call it a night.

"Team G! Look alive!" called Volleyball Coach.

We woke from our Gatorade-and-candy-induced stupors and got to our feet. I fixed my volleyball T-shirt and ensured the sleeves were properly rolled up because fashion first. We scurried to our positions in a nearly empty gym wearing ill-fitting shirts.

"No, you're over here!"

"You are definitely behind me."

"Places, everyone!" I joked.

Volleyball Coach visibly cringed at our antics.

We looked at our opposing team on the court and knew we should have left several hours ago. My direct opponent had a nose ring and wore combat boots instead of sneakers. I took that as a bad sign. The rest of the game was a blur. I missed the ball twice. I think the whole event took less than ten minutes.

In short, we walked onto the court, then quickly off. We were—I think—fine with that.

The following week, I did not attend volleyball practice.

I did not want to sit for hours in a gym for ten minutes of playing time. Nor did I want to sit in a gym for an hour. I did not want to play. I certainly did not want to participate in another game in an empty gym, humiliating myself.

A week, then two weeks, passed. I waited for Volleyball Coach to send a scathing note or call my parents saying I had stopped attending practices and games. I never received a message.

One day, I passed Volleyball Coach in the hall.

"Hi, Coach." I smiled faintly, unable to avoid her.

"Hi, there, honey." She nodded warmly and kept walking.

She either didn't notice or didn't care. I breathed in the anonymity of being on Team G. My teammates never mentioned my absence. It's as though we all pretended Team G didn't happen.

That day, I found a white envelope on our dining room table. Inside, I saw my volleyball photograph in dimensions no one needed. Dozens of pictures showed me sitting on the ground hugging a dirty volleyball in an unflattering T-shirt as a member of Cherokee Middle School's eighth grade volleyball Team G.

"Wow, the athlete's pictures finally arrived!" My mom hip-checked me and took the envelope. She pulled a glossy eight-by-ten photo out of the package.

"Should we buy a frame for it?" She held the portrait in front of us. I looked at my cheeky brace face full of optimism.

That photograph is a lie. I was not ashamed I tried out for the volleyball team; however, this photograph would lead to too many questions I did not want to answer.

"Nope. Hide it in the desk drawer with that dance picture I hate."

My Hanes unisex volleyball T-shirt was a lot like my volleyball career. No amount of tweaking and tugging would have made that shirt fit. Yet for a short time, I wanted to slip on a new identity. Without putting in time, effort, or practice, I wanted my parents and peers to see me differently and congratulate me for my athletic prowess.

Next time, I'd join something for the right reasons.

Team G taught me an important lesson. I swore I would not join clubs, groups, or cliques for other people's approval.

Unless I look great in the uniform.

Well, I wasn't perfect.

5.

SUPERWOMAN

I stood at the edge of a padded platform, swaying toward a small arena twelve feet in the air. I clipped a harness around my waist and wore a bike helmet one or two sizes too big. Bucky, an acne-covered fourteen-year-old boy, finished connecting me to a braided cord attached to a metal frame far above my head. Bucky had a buzz cut and wore Wranglers and a *sk8!* T-shirt. I knew he knew I was five seconds away from vomiting Baskin Robbins ice cream cake onto the dirt arena.

I peeked over the padded platform and saw the limestone gravel beneath me. Only sharp rocks and dirt would catch me when the cord inevitably snapped and I plummeted to my death.

The Superman was the most popular ride at the Barn Swings in Ozark, Missouri. My classmates spent the afternoon tied together in harnesses, swinging from a rope above a dirt road. Without hesitation, they tied the equivalent of a rubber band around their waists, jumped off a rickety steel contraption, and swung in circles with outstretched arms without a net, trampoline, mattress, or hay pile to break their fall. Bucky was responsible for their safety and looked more interested in his second bottle of Mountain Dew than their well-being.

I cursed birthday activities. The Superman won the title for worst birthday activity *of all time.*

I had to make a decision. Suicide attempt via Superman or public humiliation?

* * *

Typically, I love birthdays. Cake, as a rule, is my favorite food group. I do not care what culinary experts, foodies, or skinny people say. I love picking out gifts for my friends and families on their birthdays. I am thrilled to attend a themed party. Gift bags? Don't mind if I do. I say, start swag appreciation as early as possible. However, growing up, I had issues with birthday activities.

Let's review a few, shall we? Clowns. They might not be in vogue now, but in the early 1980s, parents still thought it was appropriate to incorporate clowns into birthday parties. My friend's uncle dressed like a clown for her birthday, and I was told to sit on his lap for photographs.

In a photo from her sixth birthday party, I sat on her uncle's knee while she sat on his other knee. I smiled at the camera. The smile didn't reach my eyes.

Tell your Uncle Steve to stay home with his orange wig, giant feet, and disturbing makeup. Oh, and his breath smells like Bud Light, said my eyes.

Another rite of birthday party passages was the sleepover. Between ages five and eight, I accepted invitations to sleepovers with friends and practiced my first Irish goodbyes. In my early twenties, I was known for ducking out of parties or social gatherings early without saying goodbye to anyone. This habit began when I was five years old at sleepovers.

I woke up my friends' parents in the middle of the night, asked them to call my mom, and my mom would pick me up from my friend's house. My friend would awake the following day to find me gone and was disappointed I did not stay for cartoons and pancakes. Sometimes I returned to my friend's house wearing pajamas so I could join them for pancakes. Sometimes I called it a wash and caught up on my beauty sleep.

Later, sleepovers became hostile environments. In the fourth grade, friends decided to watch *Hellraiser* for the evening entertainment. I was more of a *The Little Mermaid* or the Canadian Broadcast Company's *Anne of Green Gables* kind of girl. Rather than say no, I sat on the couch and pretended to watch the movie with my eyes closed. I reasoned that it was dark, so people might not notice.

"Mora, are your eyes closed?" the host asked while Pinhead made his grand entrance on the screen.

"Um, *no*." I laughed nervously. With my eyes closed.

Sleepovers and horror flicks were mere child's play compared to the region's most popular birthday party destination and safety hazard: The Barn Swings. It was an aptly named property composed of barns with—you guessed it—"swings" in them. This event space in a rural area frequently hosted birthday parties and youth group events. Here, one could build a bonfire and roast marshmallows. One could go on a hayride. One could eat birthday cake on picnic tables. One could cut oneself on an old mattress spring and get tetanus.

Let me explain.

The Barn Swings or Hay Swings—the name was interchangeable—was a large barn divided into several rooms. Each room was constructed with three essential components:

1. A platform: Kids and adults climbed the platform. This platform could be constructed of hay bales, wood, or, like on Superman, a metal frame. The essential goal was to climb high enough to reach the swing.
2. A swing: This apparatus hung from the center of the ceiling. I can't recall if it was rope or cord, but it dangled from the ceiling by a hook and, toward its bottom, had a sizable teardrop-shaped net. We would surround ourselves with the net and ensure we were well-seated in the teardrop-shaped loop. Then, we ran across the platform made of hay or wood, jumped off, and swung around the barn in a circular motion.

3. A soft landing: Hopefully. Depending on your room, the Barn Swings had options for your free fall to earth. In two rooms, you could fall onto hay-filled floors. Hay fever got you down? Maybe you should try the mattress room! This room was covered in old mattresses from God knows where. They had stains, dust, dirt, and probably large communities of mites, bedbugs, and fleas we didn't even know existed. Twin, full, and queen-sized mattresses were haphazardly stacked on the floor, so you bounced atop someone's old bed when you fell. No muss, no fuss. Just mind the rusty springs when you jump from the net! Those springs'll get you.

Please understand I am not disparaging rural America, hay bales, or barns. Were we roasting marshmallows outside? Great. Hayride with Dr. Pepper? Yes, and thank you. Was the county fair in town? I arrived with my 4-H group, showing off cake-decorating skills. I was, however, an anxious kid with terrible allergies and a fear of heights who found herself in a social situation where people wanted to wrap themselves in a cord and jump into a hay-filled abyss.

That did not sound like my idea of a good time.

When I arrived at the Barn Swings, I gave my frenemy, Courtney, her birthday gift. She thanked me politely because her mom monitored her social etiquette and showed me to the Barn's Hay Room.

Instantly, my allergies sprang to life. A thin river of clear mucus immediately ran out of my nose. I tried to sniff and snort inconspicuously because that seemed more appropriate than using the back of my sleeve to wipe it away in front of the birthday girl.

Hoping to distract Courtney, I offered her my New Kids on the Block and Paula Abdul cassettes to play on the stereo I noticed when I arrived. I loved Paula Abdul and recently developed a dance routine loosely based on her "Straight Up" video.

"Oh, no. They only play Christian rock here." Courtney side-eyed my latest Laker-Girl-sinner-gone-mainstream music. Ashamed, I stuffed it in my jeans pocket.

"Oh, sure. I guess I forgot."

Only Christian rock? I had no idea.

"Anyway, do you know how to do this?" Courtney threw her thumb over her shoulder toward the barn and its infamous swings.

"I think so."

Again, I had no idea.

"Well, some of us are doing the Superman. People are pairing up!" Courtney announced.

She and her older sister's high school friends walked outside to take advantage of *the* ride. The granddaddy of all Barn Swings. I walked outside the dim barn and witnessed the most terrifying sight. Two girls I knew from school were strapped together with what looked like a glorified seat belt, side by side, wearing helmets. They were attached to cords that hung from a metal frame. These young girls swung from their stomachs in the air without a net to catch them.

"What are Lindsey and Jessica doing?" I squeaked. I turned my eyes as another teenager pushed them onto a small platform further into the arena.

"One! Two!" they counted simultaneously. I didn't see or hear the rest. I shut my eyes. When I opened them, Lindsey and Jessica squealed with outstretched arms as they "flew" like Superman.

"Is everyone doing this?" Panic immediately set in. I didn't hear a response because my heartbeat was uproarious in my ears. No way was I going through with this. Buddy system or not, my fear of heights usually influenced the majority of my decisions, and I didn't see that changing today.

"People don't have to do it, but it's super fun." Courtney watched my response.

She's throwing down the gauntlet, and she knows it.

"My sisters love it and say it's not even scary. I think Heather and I are going to do it next," she bragged.

"Awesome," I said noncommittally.

My eyes were still on the sky. Lindsey and Jessica lost momentum, and Bucky—the teenager—eased them to the ground and pulled off their gear. My friends surrounded the girls like they were heroes returning from a space mission.

"It was so amazing up there." Jessica tried to sound like this ride suddenly gave her a newfound perspective on the sixth grade. "You feel really small, and the world is so big."

Barf.

"I'm so glad we could do that together!" Jessica hugged Lindsey.

Ugh, liar. She couldn't stand the sight of Lindsey yesterday because she started wearing Eternity perfume, and Jessica wore Eternity perfume first. *Besides, we all know you stole your mom's travel-sized bottle from her purse.*

The Superman frenzy began. A parade of partygoers paired up to attempt the swing. They waited in line, putting on their gear, and I made myself as scarce as possible. Suddenly, I was invested in prepping the bonfire, setting the picnic table for cake, and checking in with Courtney's mom on her recent PTA president nomination.

"That's so exciting!" I gushed as I followed her mom toward the cake and away from the Superman. I looked for any reason to be helpful and unavailable.

After everyone ate cake and played the last Christian rock album, the jig was up.

"Mora, you didn't get to do the Superman yet, did you?" Courtney tested.

"No," I hedged. "That's okay. If someone else wants to go—"

"We've all gone, I think," the good hostess offered. "It's your turn."

Standing on the Superman platform, I took stock of the situation.

I had a swollen red nose and sore throat from my allergic reaction to hay.

My body hurt from falling into and onto hay for most of the afternoon.

I had arrived with gifts, music, and good intentions.

Why must I endure physical and mental torture to celebrate someone else's birthday?

A few people on the ground looked at me. Courtney whispered something into Heather's ear while keeping her eyes on me. I scanned the crowd, but no one in that crowd would save me. Even Courtney's mom was back by the bonfire, so the power of the PTA couldn't save me now.

Usually, Courtney's gesture would be enough to unravel me, and I'd do anything in my power to avoid being a topic of gossip. But my fear of heights, snotty nose, and dull bodily pain finally usurped social demands. I made my decision.

"Nope." I shook my head.

"Huh?" Bucky suddenly came to.

"Bring me back, Bucky," I demanded.

With his foot, Bucky pulled back the padded ledge to the leading platform and unhooked my harness. I tentatively walked backward, holding onto Bucky—gross—until I was close enough to the central platform. Instead of walking off the platform and climbing the nearby ladder, I got as close to the ground as humanly possible while still in the air. I hit the deck and slid backward on my stomach, feeling my way to the escape route. I eased toward the ladder and carefully climbed down until my feet met solid ground.

Catching my breath, I walked like John Wayne, due to the big harness between my legs, away from the Superman. I did not wait for Bucky to help me take my equipment off. I wanted to put as much room between me and that nightmare of a swing first.

"Didn't you want to do the Superman?" Courtney looked at me with big, innocent eyes.

"No. I never wanted to do the Superman."

Lindsey and Jessica snickered at my response and watched me waddle away. My red nose, chafed thighs, sore throat, and hay-filled hair likely looked horrifying to everyone at the party—Courtney's high school-aged sister, her mother, Bucky, and even Jessica and Lindsey.

I did not care.

I did not think it was unreasonable to be nervous about jumping off a ride managed by a teen without a safety net beneath me. That was not neurotic behavior. I pretended to enjoy clowns, sleepovers at strange houses, horror movies, and even subjected myself to a day of allergic reactions. After being tortured at birthday parties for years, I finally said no. I looked my captors in the eye and said, "No cake was worth this anguish."

Despite the equipment weighing me down, I felt like I could fly for the first time that day.

When my mom picked me up from the birthday party, she noticed my disheveled appearance. "Mora, are you okay? What happened?" She looked concerned. "Did you have any fun at all?"

"The barn rooms with the hay swings were fun," I admitted. "Mom, I need some Benadryl when we go home."

"Sure thing, hon." She nodded. "Well, I'm glad you gave it a shot."

However, I knew the bigger accomplishment was what I did not do that day.

By saying no to Superman, I became Superwoman.

6.

MAKING HISTORY

Growing up, athletic coaches and I did not communicate well.

I responded to words of affirmation and opportunities for personal expression. At my high school, the coaches I knew did not speak that love language. Many athletic coaches taught academic classes and treated their classrooms like playing fields and their students like teams. They gave instructions in clipped dialogue. They wore windbreakers and chinos and carried whistles.

History Coach was no exception. Unfortunately, everyone knew his honors US History class was required if you wanted to kick-start the advanced curriculum. I was hell-bent on getting an A in History Coach's class to ensure my first-year GPA was rock solid. I knew I could not run track, but his class would not impede my academic track record.

Toward the end of our semester, History Coach announced the final project. If we received full marks on the project, he would submit it to a regional History Day competition where unnamed judges bestowed winners with prizes like trophies and ribbons with the prestigious title, "History Day 1996."

History Coach spoke with reverence about History Day and the boundless opportunities this could bring to our academic careers.

"For example," he said, showing us a glossy photo of a sophomore named Holly Stewart. "Holly here dressed up like Queen Elizabeth I and gave a presentation as though she was the queen herself," he said, beaming with pride.

Holly Stewart was, objectively, a perfect person. A varsity cheerleader, class officer, and honors student, Holly Stewart was difficult to ignore and, even worse, easy to like.

History Coach passed around the picture of Holly dressed in Elizabethan finery, standing in the high school cafeteria during what was, presumably, History Day. Her bounty of auburn hair was wrapped on her head and styled so she looked like a portrait from the Albert and Victoria Museum halls. She was impressive, and I understood why she was such a success story. I assumed Holly's spectacular showing at History Day also impacted History Coach's reputation on the regional history teacher circuit.

I might not be able to run a mile in less than eight minutes. Or ten minutes. *But I'm the next History Day queen.*

I decided to develop a History Day entry that would solidify my GPA's place in the succession of History Day royalty.

Some of you may be wondering why Elizabeth I had such a prominent role in US History class. I think what's important is that Holly Stewart had auburn hair, and Queen Elizabeth I wore red wigs.

So let's not ask ridiculous questions, okay?

At home, I updated Mom on History Day.

Strategy #1: Reinforce History Coach's reputation.

"He's tough, Mom," I said with resignation. "This is the first of several difficult honors courses that will kick-start my high school career."

I likened the classes to the obstacles between Indiana Jones and the Holy Grail in *The Last Crusade*—just one battle after another. My mother was competitive and typically willing to be my co-conspirator when it came to grades.

Strategy #2: Appeal to Mom's competitive side.

"This will make up a significant part of my grade, so I must take it that extra mile," I prepped. "You know, last year, Holly won a regional History Day competition." This piqued my mom's interest.

"Oh?" she asked. My mom loved a post-school day dish session. She wanted details, names, and a success story. She was prepped to compete.

"Yeah," I continued. "She dressed like Queen Elizabeth I of England and gave a presentation as the queen about her reign as one of the most successful monarchs in Europe. And women in history."

That's right. My strategy included a subtle sprinkle of girl power to seal the deal. I needed a costume and didn't have costume funds. If my oratory required some girl power, so be it.

"Well, you can't be Elizabeth I too," my mom, ever the pragmatist, reasoned.

Sigh. Of course I couldn't be Elizabeth. I wasn't asking for a lame copycat strategy. I was annoyed. *Don't lose your cool.*

"No. Of course not," I agreed, politely. "I need a fresh idea with the power of Elizabeth I, but, you know, 'Make it Mora.'" I tried to sell this concept with jazz hands.

"I don't know where we're going to get a costume, and I can't sew anything complicated," she noted.

Victory! She's in.

Her wheels were fully cranking. She was engaged in this ridiculousness now, too. Even better? She was thinking in terms of what she could or could not sew.

I thought we'd rent a costume. But now I'll get a custom outfit? This was next-level devotion to education and artistry.

"Let's think about it," she bought herself some time.

Strategy 3: Play it cool.

"Sure. Absolutely," I said. "Take all the time you need."

Like any good Midwestern mafioso, I knew when to push and when to stand back. I'd give her a day. Then I'd bring her the list of ideas I already developed.

These ideas included:

- Abigail Adams, because I always loved her "Remember the Ladies" letter to John Adams.
- Dolley Madison, First Lady and widely considered an arts preservationist.
- Louisa May Alcott, because I was obsessed with the March sisters in *Little Women*. Okay. I am still obsessed with the March sisters in *Little Women*.

Despite the strict gender norms each of these women had to subscribe to, they influenced political and social change in their time. Also, every option guaranteed I would wear an impressive gown and tell a tale that would tug on the heartstrings of patriots throughout the region. I was always strategic when it came to the dramatic impact of a performance.

Cue the waterworks, everyone.

I prepared to make history.

"I think I have an idea," Mom said after dinner that night. I sat on my bed and turned off The Cranberries' *No Need to Argue* CD and tuned in to my mom's latest inspiration.

"Oh?" I asked.

I love her enthusiasm.

"What about Mother Teresa?" She beamed.

Everything screeched to a halt. I heard my heartbeat. My carefully executed strategy slowly crumbled, and I tried to capture the pieces.

"'Scuse me?" I looked confused.

"Mother Teresa. I can't sew, but I could make a sari like nuns in her order wear. It's a simple design. Then we would need to learn the proper way to fasten it," she said earnestly. My mother went to Catholic school and always had a soft spot for nuns, missionary work, and social justice.

"But, um, it's for US History?" My mind scrambled to rebalance itself after this recommendation.

"That doesn't seem to matter if Holly was Elizabeth I," countered Mom.

Cunning, Mother. Well-played.

I was hesitant to bypass my original prospects, though. I liked the idea of Abigail, Dolley, or Louisa. Their means of influence despite societal gender norms, their spheres of influence, and those hoopskirts.

I also knew I was being unreasonable. Asking too much of my mom. It was my project, after all.

Ugh. Building a hoopskirt would be impossible or expensive.

"She's also a nun," I pointed out. That was my last hand. If that didn't work, I was prepared to fold.

"Mora, you can explain what a nun is to your class," Mom confirmed. Nuns and Catholicism were a tough sell in southwest Missouri. Southern Baptists and Evangelists dominated the region and had a church on every block. Catholics got a bad rap for focusing on Mary and involving too many saints in prayers. Like we organized a party and let the guest list get out of control.

Hey. Don't you want to go on a date in high school? Why are you considering dressing like Mother Teresa for a public high school class when no one has asked you to wear a costume? Why are you determined to commit social suicide so early in your high school career?

The need to fit in to the upper echelon of scholars blinded me. This was the option put before me. Go big or go home.

I folded.

"Should I practice an Albanian accent?" I asked shakily.

* * *

For the next month, I developed a report about Mother Teresa and typed it on my father's desktop computer. Like many Gen X and Millennial cuspers, I conducted my research on Microsoft Encarta and at the library. Dial-up internet was a debacle, so I rarely researched information on the World Wide Web. I also borrowed my dad's slide projector that he used when teaching his art courses. That's right, I made a literal slideshow about Mother Teresa's life. I planned to read my report with the accompanying slideshow, dressed as Mother Teresa.

Academics meets performance art.

My mother fashioned a "sari," which I'm sure was not a sari and would probably be considered offensive if I lived anywhere else in the country at any later time. My mom placed Velcro on any spot on the long piece of material that might need securing. Wearing the costume was more of an art than a science, but it was directionally accurate, and there was no mistaking who I was trying to portray.

To complete my transformation, I did practice an Albanian accent.

Why not push this over the top and make it as uncomfortable as possible and borderline offensive for everyone forced to witness this train wreck? Why wouldn't the fifteen-year-old Caucasian girl from Springfield, Missouri, stand up in her US History class dressed as a nun and pretend she was Albanian? She wants to participate in an academic competition. That's why! She wants an A! She wants to secure her role as a smart kid.

Some may describe this behavior as extra, cringe, thirsty, desperate, or inappropriate. They would be right.

The day of my presentation finally came. Before my freshman honors US History class, I changed into my costume in one of the girls' bathroom stalls.

I'll wait until the bell rings, and then I'll run to class in my Mother Teresa costume. I don't want upperclassmen to see me and think I'm weird or anything.

At this point, I was beyond weird.

As the bell stopped ringing, I slipped into the classroom with a slide projector in tow. My costume could only be described as a giant dish towel secured with Velcro straps over boot-cut jeans and platform sandals with a purple JanSport backpack. I looked like Baby Spice wrapped in an ill-fitted dishcloth.

I stopped in the classroom's doorway, expecting to see other History Day enthusiasts in their costumes. Instead, it grew quiet as my peers, looking at me curiously, walked to their desks. They carried reports bound in clear covers. Some had trifold boards entitled "Civil Rights in the 1960s" or "The Gettysburg Address."

No one else wore a costume. No one else held a slide projector in a leather case from the 1950s. No one else, I assure you, had been practicing an Albanian accent that week.

But no one looked more stunned than History Coach. His eyebrows drew together as he watched me take my seat, uncertain about how the next ninety minutes of his life would unfold. He tried to avoid my gaze, but I sat in the front row and watched him carefully. He attempted to cover his face, but I saw him stifle a laugh and wipe tears from his eyes. As I waited in my makeshift sari, History Coach took a moment to gather himself.

"Everyone, have a seat. Let's take a minute or two to, uh, get ourselves together," he addressed the class.

Nice. Subtle. Here I was, ready to pour my heart and soul into a presentation about a deeply religious woman and human rights activist, and this guy was laughing at me.

I seethed.

I may not have auburn hair and a golden gown; however, I showed up with reams of robust biographical information and heart, thank you very much.

I was humiliated and considered returning to the bathroom, taking off my sari, and handing in my report. But what was the use? Everyone saw me. I was in too deep.

Then, I thought of my mom. My mother, who hated sewing, sewed this for me. I thought of Mother Teresa—a poor

Albanian woman who selflessly gave to the poor, cared for the sick, and put herself at risk time and time again for the greater good. Who told people they could bring happiness to the world if they loved their families. I was ashamed the only women I initially thought to discuss were privileged white women who used their social status to influence change. Here was a woman who had nothing but gave everything because she gave herself.

A new determination settled in me. I was going to be amazing. I was going to be the best Mother Teresa anyone ever saw. When my name was called, I dimmed the lights, secured my sari, turned on the slide projector, and began my speech with a vague Albanian accent.

Click-click.

"My name is Mother Teresa. I was born in Albania, the youngest of three children."

Click-click.

Kids avoided eye contact with me and pretended to be interested in anything except this scene. They drew on their desktops and wrote and rewrote their names in notebooks. They tried not to dwell on the girl who would probably not attend homecoming that year; they were right, I did not.

Some stared at me, too stunned to look away. These voyeurs stopped smacking their Bubble Tape to lean over their desks and peer at me like I was an animal at the zoo. They studied me, trying to understand my behavior and what would motivate me to make such a spectacle of myself in a public setting.

A couple of childhood friends gave me thumbs-up with encouraging smiles, full of silver braces decorated with multicolored bands. They were either as delusional as I was or just really supportive.

History Coach stood in the corner of the classroom, shrouded in darkness. I think he kept to the shadows while I gave my slide presentation to hide his laughter. I couldn't swear to it, but his red face and watery eyes when I completed my presentation were a hint.

Click-click.

"Mora, I promise you were amazing," Cristen, my best friend and soul sister, told me later. "He spends all his time with athletes, and it's important that he's exposed to creativity." She had known me since I was two years old. Cristen was—and still is—a generous optimist. And maybe my enabler.

"Oh my gosh. Are you sure? I think he was seriously laughing at me," I rambled. "Do you think he got it? I need 100 percent if I'm going to the regional History Day competition and then getting a solid A in the class. If I don't get an A in this class, my weighted GPA will be a mess and—"

"Don't worry about that," said Cristen.

We squeezed through the congested halls on our way to our next class. "You know he'll make you work a little harder than the athletes, but he also has a soft spot for the creatives. Plus, you were the only one in costume. Gotta get to band," she noted reassuringly.

As Cristen hauled her giant French horn toward the band room, I gratefully nodded and promised to keep her updated. Then, I attempted to speed walk in my platform sandals to biology.

Thanks to Cristen and our short exchange, hope sprang eternal.

Several weeks later, History Coach returned our reports and presentations. Those with 100 percent grades would participate in the regional History Day competition. When I received my written report, I eagerly flipped through the pages, anxiously awaiting the verdict.

"Ninety-eight percent. Mother Theresa is not American. Congratulations on the most memorable History Day entry to date!" History Coach wrote in bright red ink.

Ninety-eight percent? Where did those two points go? Did he take two points off my grade in US History for not highlighting someone in US History? Since when was that in the rule book? And why two points? Why that arbitrary number? All those hours at night repeating Mother Teresa's interviews so I could be more comfortable with unique syntax . . . and for *what*? Holly Stewart wasn't penalized for this!

The injustice of it all struck me in the stomach.

That was it. I would not go to History Day and be considered one of the great historians known throughout Springfield, Missouri, in the year of our Lord 1996.

I steamed. I fumed. I ate a Bagel Bite and drank Diet Pepsi. I watched Oprah. It was how I processed.

I realized several things: I could have cleared my History Day topic with History Coach before diving into a one-woman show. I could have done the work myself and not involved Mom. I could have learned about something I liked without being focused on winning History Day. I was interested in the Revolutionary War, women going to work during World War II, and the Industrial Revolution.

Why didn't I just do the assignment?

I tried to emulate someone else and focused on their success. Not my own or what was important to me. Do you know who didn't do that? Abigail Adams, Dolley Madison, Louisa Alcott, and Mother Teresa. With this realization, I sheepishly slipped my sari onto a hanger and placed it in the back of my closet.

Three and a half years later, I replaced the Mother Teresa sari in my closet with a golden high school graduation gown. I did receive an A in US Honors History class, even if I didn't make it to History Day. However, it was not the gateway to an "upper echelon" of scholastic aptitude. Upon receiving my grade, I was not welcomed into the

Dead Poet's Society. No one gave me a blazer, showed me a handshake, or welcomed me into a lounge to sip on cognac beneath oil paintings. Instead, I enrolled in more honors classes throughout high school. Talk about anticlimactic.

While my Mother Teresa History Day presentation was over-the-top and misguided, I can confidently say I did carpe diem. Ultimately, I'm proud I was the "most memorable entry to date" and not just another History Day participant. Because sometimes, I think, that's how history is made.

7.

LATE BLOOMER

When it came to romance, I was a late bloomer. Maybe because my first date included a blooming butterfly garden and a police arrest.

I was a teen in the nineties who liked speech and debate, improv, academics, and poetry; therefore, my version of romantic relationships often included confusing friendships in which I eventually learned my friend had feelings for me at an embarrassing moment, or I harbored romantic feelings for someone I swore was "just a friend." For years.

This inevitably culminated in someone initiating conversations like "Hey, um, can we talk about something?" or "Your friendship has become *really* important to me." Spoiler alert: these conversations never ended in a romantic relationship.

Another classic scenario involved hanging out in groups with unnecessary people to buffer the interaction with your object of desire. Maybe you talked to them. Maybe you didn't. Welcome to the world of the romantically inept.

By my senior year of high school, I decided I needed dating experience before college. I thought my college experience would mirror Felicity Porter's—the namesake character on the WB's hit show *Felicity* (Abrams and Reeves 1998–2002). I anticipated being caught in so many romances, including those with brooding residence advisors and former high school heroes, that I needed a crash course in what to expect when it came to dating. How would I concentrate on my studio art classes if I had to deal with so many confusing relationships?

Sidebar: I didn't need to worry because I would not live in an edgy, coed fine arts dorm in New York City like Felicity; instead, I lived in a limestone gothic all-girls dorm at the University of Missouri-Columbia nicknamed "the convent."

But I digress.

I learned about relationships from *Jane Eyre*, *Anne of Green Gables*, Jane Austen, and my mom's Nora Roberts romance novels. Based on this research, I needed to become a governess, walk the ridgepole of a school roof, obtain a dowry, or return to my hometown and reconnect with the rancher/farmer/sailor/teacher/chef who was my nemesis and secret love.

"I need a dating strategy," I told my friend Cristen. We cleaned offices every weekend for extra money, but before dusting and scrubbing, we drank Diet Dr. Peppers and ate Thin Mints.

"Okay," she said slowly, willing to hear me out.

"I haven't really dated anyone or had a serious relationship, right?" I said, just getting started. "So I need to date someone who doesn't go to our school and is funny."

"Why can't he go to our school?" she asked.

"Well, I'm not really interested in anyone at school," I said. "Also, if things go sideways, I don't have to see or talk to him."

"Why do you think it's going to fall apart?" Cristen asked. I loved her. She was such an optimist—the yin to my yang.

"It's just a precaution," I reasoned.

She laughed. "And 'funny' is the other quality?" she said, looking at me questioningly. "That's it?"

"Time is of the essence," I said. "We're graduating soon. I can't be weighed down by too many criteria. Bonus points for someone nice, presentable, or going to college."

"You do like a jokester." She smiled.

"I really do," I said. "Now, let's see how quickly I can dust this office."

I wasn't into the bad boy trope. Funny, yes. Bad, no. The inside of my locker and notebooks included inkjet prints of Chris O'Donnell, Adam Sandler, and Matt Damon because, even then, Ben Affleck seemed a little unpredictable. Breaking rules made me nervous; I was a horrible liar and would be caught if I attempted anything. If I lied, my eyes darted everywhere; I rambled, immediately apologized, and told the truth. My friends avoided telling me about their more delinquent activities because they knew I was a liability.

So I looked for a funny and nice guy who would ease me into dating.

I set my eyes on Brian because he ticked the boxes: different school and funny. We had mutual friends through school activities, and he always seemed up to some antics, making people laugh. Bonus: he had nice eyes and looked relatively clean. He was going away to college that fall. Without a Mr. Rochester, Gilbert Blythe, or Mr. Darcy available on speed dial, he seemed like a safe bet.

I dropped hints that I was interested in Brian by telling absolutely *all* of our mutual friends I wanted him to call me. Please. Now. Thanks. I may have struggled with balancing that nuanced area between total avoidance and stalking people, but, you know, there's a learning curve with these things.

First, we communicated for several weeks via AOL instant messenger. Oh, the sweet sound of "You've got mail." The ping of a message! The swinging door sound of someone joining the AOL IM platform! These were the moments in the late 1990s for which savvy tech teens lived. We saw each other almost every weekend at school activities.

Then one day, the house phone rang. Brian called me.

Maybe he felt he had nowhere to hide. Maybe everyone in our mutual social circle urged him to do so. Or maybe he couldn't resist a fellow speech nerd who knew how to wear a denim dress and jaunty silk neck scarf. Who could blame him?

Some friends and family were not thrilled about my burgeoning relationship.

I thought my parents would be pleased I dated in speech and debate circles; however, Brian put my parents on high alert.

"I don't trust him," my dad grumbled. My dad did not trust many teenage boys, but he was exceptionally watchful with Brian. Dad simply didn't take to this younger version of Dan Quayle on his doorstep.

My little sister, Sarah, who I regarded as my moral compass, also disliked him.

"Well . . . what do you think?" I asked excitedly, hoping for some sisterly girl talk.

"No. I don't like him," said Sarah, without preamble. She immediately crushed any heart-to-heart chat I hoped to have with her.

"What's wrong with him?" I asked, feeling disappointed and sounding defensive.

"This one's trouble." My sister could turn from a sweet-faced twelve-year-old to a surly movie cop circa 1946. She may as well have had a cigar hanging out of her mouth. "I don't like the look of him."

"Oh my God," I said, exasperated.

Even his friends expressed some concern.

"Are you sure about this? Dating Brian?" they asked, skeptically. "He's, uh, gone out with a few people this year."

"Erm, we just went out a couple of times," I said, awkwardly. "I'm not marrying him." While I appreciated their protectiveness, it seemed like strange behavior. Weren't guys supposed to support each other? Bro codes or something?

He goes to another school, and he's funny. I'm dating someone. This is what I want. Right?

* * *

"Let's get our drinks to go," Brian said. "I've been working on a project, and I'd like to show it to you."

"Where is it?" I asked.

"It's a surprise," he said.

Brian looked at me eagerly, and I felt two distinct emotions: I was happy he planned something special for our date. But I was nervous because this was how most *Law & Order* (Wolf 1990) episodes began.

"Okay, sure." I smiled politely. I found my Lip Smacker lip gloss in my messenger bag and reapplied. I did not know what to expect and always reapplied my Lip Smackers when I was nervous.

Brian drove to my old elementary school. He went to the far end of the parking lot and stopped the car near the school entrance and playground.

"What are we doing at my old school?" I asked uncertainly. As an avid rule follower, my alarm bells were already going off.

"I want to show you what I made," he said. "Come here."

He took my hand, and we walked to long garden plots neatly outfitted with blond wood. I spotted burgeoning flowers breaking through new, black soil.

"It's a butterfly garden. I made it in Scouts. It mostly attracts monarchs. Since it's at your old school, I thought you'd like to see it."

"Brian, this is awesome. You did this?"

I liked the idea of butterflies visiting the little kids at my old elementary school. The garden replaced an empty spot in the old playground, previously covered in dust and dirt. I was thrilled to know one day it would be filled with flowers and floating butterflies.

"It's so pretty," I said, continuing to look at the plot.

"Good. I'm glad you like it." He seemed pleased with the compliment, retook my hand, and led me back to the car.

I felt giddy. I was touched Brian participated in community service, remembered my elementary school, and shared the experience with me. The garden tugged at my sappy heartstrings, and I lowered my guard.

Inside the car, I buckled my seat belt and waited for Brian to start the car.

"Look, I want you to know how I feel about you," he said after a long pause.

Uh-oh. Please don't ruin this. I began to sweat.

Then, he leaned back into his seat and looked at the sky, taking a breath. After a dramatic pause, he turned his head toward me.

"I luu... luuuu..." he stuttered, unable to speak.

"What?" I asked, indelicately.

"I luuu..." he tried again.

Before he could complete the sentence, the headlights of a nondescript black sedan briefly shone on us. Then, the car slowly turned left and onto the main road. The brief interruption provided a reprieve, and I exhaled.

Brian looked momentarily annoyed. Then, he determinedly resumed the conversation. "I love you," he said, no longer hesitant. He waited for me to respond.

What the—? What? No. Wait. What? Does he really love me? I wasn't cynical, but this seemed unlikely. I supposed it was possible. In my heart of hearts, I wanted to believe someone loved me.

He's, uh, gone out with a few people this year. I heard the warning in my head. He seemed unlikely to go from *like* to *love* in a few short weeks. So I responded with the most cringe-worthy cop-out known to man.

"Aw. Thank you," I said, aware I sounded cold and lame. I smiled and touched his arm in an effort to be comforting.

At that horrible moment, the black sedan returned to the parking lot. The driver beamed its headlights on us and stopped the car. Without saying a word, Brian started his car, turned it to face the sedan, and revved the engine.

"Brian? What are you doing?" I asked. I clutched the car's sides and pressed my right foot to the floor the way my mom reactively tried to brake when she accompanied me on driving lessons.

Brian stopped paying attention to me. Without warning, he stepped on the gas and drove straight toward the sedan, playing some insane game of chicken.

My tombstone would say, "Death by Dating." I shut my eyes, convinced I was about to die.

At the last moment, Brian swerved, narrowly missing the dark sedan. He stopped his vehicle and paused before driving into the main street.

That's when the policeman turned on his unmarked car's lights.

"What have you kids been drinkin'?" yelled the policeman.

"Earl Grey iced tea," I cried earnestly. I showed him my mostly empty iced tea cup.

He took Brian out of the car and handcuffed him. I couldn't see Brian or talk to him.

"Oh yeah? Whadda you have in yer bag, missy? Doobies?"

I turned my bag upside down to reveal its contents. The most emo-nerd combination of purse items rolled out of my Gap messenger bag, including Lip Smacker lip gloss, a Velcro-enclosed wallet, a paperback copy of J. D. Salinger's *Franny and Zooey*, my 1988 Dodge Daytona car keys, a house key, and a small 1940s vintage compact mirror. Edgy stuff.

"It's a good thing I saw you were in the car with him," he said. "'Cause I was about to shoot. What were you two thinking?"

This policeman was in full cowboy mode and was ready to intimidate me as much as possible.

"I don't know." I continued to cry. "He showed me the butterfly garden, told me he loved me, and then lost his mind."

I almost hoped the police officer would explain what in the world had transpired. However, this was not a sage policeman who would tell me the world's ways. He was amped up and prepared to read a cocky teenager his rights.

"Are your parents home?" he asked instead.

"Yes," I said.

"Good. You got a quarter?" he asked.

"I think so," I said. I dug into my Velcro wallet and looked for loose change.

"Then walk down to the gas station, call yer mama and daddy, and have them come get you. I'm taking your friend with me," he said.

"You want me to walk to the gas station? It's dark, and I'm alone. Is Brian going to jail? I don't understand," I said.

"Just get them to pick you up," he said.

I gathered my things, left the parking lot, and walked to the fluorescent lights of the nearest Fast n' Friendly gas station. With a shaking hand, I found a pay phone and called my parents. Between sobs, I asked them to pick me up and end the worst date in the world.

My mom picked me up and tried to calm me down. At home, my furious father paced around the living room. I sat on my parent's bed, cried, and told them everything.

The next day, my parents fielded communications with Brian's parents and lawyers. During that time, I learned Brian's parents picked him up at the police station. They asked whether I was okay and requested I not mention the incident because he was headed to a tournament that week and a premiere college that fall. They would reach out to lawyers about the next steps.

I provided the police and Brian's lawyers with statements about what happened that night. I was not allowed to speak with Brian until "everything was settled." I felt scared. I kept the secret. I had nightmares about the police lights. I never went back to my elementary school.

I learned Brian went to a tournament the morning after our date. At the tournament, he fell in "luuuuuve" with another girl.

Resilient guy.

* * *

That July, Brian called me and wanted to meet. Our senior year was over, and we would go to different colleges in less than a month. I knew this chapter would close soon, so I agreed to meet him.

"I'm glad we have a chance to talk," he said. We sat in his car. Again. This time, it was a church parking lot.

Are we seriously in another parking lot?

"Open the glove box," he said.

I was dubious, but I opened it anyway. Inside I saw two velvet jewelry boxes.

"What are those?" I asked, looking at him out of the corner of my eye.

"Open them. They're for you," he said, smiling.

Who was this guy? Why was an eighteen-year-old kid taking cues from villains in mid-1980s Wall Street–based movies and television shows? I opened the boxes. One contained a yellow gold bracelet—each link in the shape of a heart. The second contained golden heart earrings with heart garnets in their centers.

I guess this was how Brian "talked."

"Wow," I said, genuinely confused.

What were these? Were they "I'm sorry, and good luck with college" gifts? "I'm sorry and can we still date?" gifts? "Thanks for dealing with my legal team" gifts?

What did he think heart jewelry would solve? Had he ever cared about me in the first place?

One thing was for sure, if he thought jewelry usurped kindness and communication, he didn't know me at all.

"These are way too much, Brian. What are they for?" I finally asked.

"They're for you. You deserve them," said Brian.

How should I decode these mixed messages? Hearts symbolize love and affection, but "You deserve them" sounded like "You put in a lot of time and effort, so I'm rewarding you with jewelry."

"We're going to college soon—pretty far away from one another," I said, testing the waters. "It would be difficult to do the long-distance thing."

"Oh yeah," he said, confirming my suspicion that he was *not* interested in a serious relationship. "Totally agree."

"Totally," I said.

I assumed he liked me and felt guilty. This gift helped him feel less guilty. *Ugh.* Why was communicating with men so difficult? Why was *dating* so difficult?

I was confused, tired, and ready to retire from dating.

"Well, thank you," I told him for a second time that summer. I wanted to go home, watch movies, and cuddle my dog.

"You're welcome," he said, quickly kissing me. "I'll drive you home. I bet you'll want to call your friends and tell them about the jewelry."

Oh, for the love.

* * *

Later that week, Dad and I took a trip to the local jeweler. I approached a gleaming glass counter, and a friendly middle-aged woman greeted my father and me.

"My daughter would like to exchange some jewelry," Dad said. The woman looked surprised and turned her attention to me.

"Do you have a receipt, honey?" she asked brightly.

"No, I don't," I said. I could tell the shop assistant was about to tell me I could not make a return.

"A guy I dated gave them to me a couple days ago," I explained. "You see, he felt bad because he told me he loved me, was arrested, and cheated on me. Like in a bad country song."

The woman looked at me, my father, and then back at me.

"Do you wanna pick out something new, or would you prefer the cash?" she asked.

As my dad and I left the jeweler, he placed his hand on my shoulder.

"I like this ring better," I said. "Don't you?" I showed him the new garnet ring I wore. I exchanged the heart jewelry for something simple. Something more me. "I'm never dating again, Dad." I watched my feet as I walked.

"Well, you might," he said, thoughtfully. "But no rush, okay?"

"Yeah," I said, and it was an oath. "No rush."

I decided grand romantic gestures were overrated. I decided to change my approach to dating. Next time, I would add criteria beyond "doesn't go to my school" and "is funny." I should include things like "is kind," or "does not put me in immediate danger," and I could be more flexible with my timelines.

It could all wait. Like the butterfly garden, I still had some growing to do.

8.

HOMETOWN INTERN

One decade before *Mad Men* aired and the world met Peggy Olson, a smart and ambitious copywriter played by actress Elizabeth Moss, I decided to write copy at an advertising agency. I wanted to write pithy headlines, collaborate with designers, and pitch big ideas to clients to help them see their products and services in a new light.

I studied strategic communications at the University of Missouri's school of journalism in Columbia, but I needed to practice copywriting at an ad agency. The summer after my sophomore year of college, I felt increased pressure to get a stellar copywriting internship at a well-known agency.

Many students went to nearby cities where they had friends, parents' friends, or connections close to home. The heavy hitters were accepted into programs on the coasts, including in New York, Boston, Los Angeles, and Washington, DC. As far as I was concerned, these internships were in Greenland or on Jupiter. My hometown of Springfield was three hours from the closest metropolitan areas in Missouri—St. Louis and Kansas City. I didn't have city connections, so working and living in St. Louis, Kansas City, Chicago, or Little Rock like many of my classmates was also unlikely. I didn't entertain these opportunities and focused on Springfield, my hometown and summer destination.

That May, when I almost gave up hope on an internship, I received a lead from Mike, the husband of my sister's high school orchestra instructor, who knew someone who "did some advertising."

Wow. What a small world!

"Nowadays, he primarily works for a printing manufacturer, but I think he still does some freelance," said Mike. "He might have a couple of projects this summer and need help."

"Thank you *so much*, Mike," I said gratefully. This was the beginning of my career, and I owed him everything.

After receiving Chip's number, I didn't hesitate to call him. I left him a message, sent him a follow-up email, and attached my résumé and cover letter from my Hotmail account. Several days later, Chip Johnson agreed to take me as his apprentice. His protégé. His unpaid summer intern.

I'm in advertising, baby!

After my semester ended, I drove from Columbia, Missouri, through the Lake of the Ozarks and south toward Springfield. I counted my blessings and prepared to leap into that wild and wacky world of advertising.

That Monday, I donned my favorite Anne Klein wrap dress from Marshall's because I was determined to make a good impression, and everyone knows poly-blend wrap dresses don't wrinkle. I drove my Dodge Daytona—the automobile equivalent of a mullet—to a white tin warehouse.

I entered the building and introduced myself to a dubious-looking woman in her mid-forties who didn't get the memo about my arrival.

"Hi, I'm Mora Thompson," I said, extending my hand. "I'm here to see Chip Johnson. I'm his new intern."

The woman had dyed her hair auburn brown with shagged shoulder-length layers. The environment said "warehouse," but her eye makeup said "Studio 54" because her eyes glistened with blue eyeshadow and coats of inky mascara. The 1980s were obviously the best years of her life, and she was reluctant to let them go.

"He didn't mention you," she said after a long pause. She tapped her nails on the desk and assessed my outfit, comparing my cheap poly-blend sundress to her cheap poly-blend blouse-and-skirt set.

"Oh, well, we just solidified the arrangements a couple of weeks ago," I said, trying to be polite but realizing I didn't owe her an explanation.

She must have decided I posed a minimal threat because she directed me to the back—somewhere beyond the office space and deep into the warehouse.

Beyond the double doors was a musty, cavernous room with uninsulated walls. Giant machines moved back and forth, hauling large boxes filled with printers, paper, and copiers. Years later, despite my affinity for Kathy Bates, I never liked season six of *The Office* episodes when Sabre bought Dunder Mifflin (Krasinski 2010). I did not realize why until I remembered *that moment*. Middle-aged men stared at me—the nineteen-year-old woman wandering through the warehouse in her cheap sundress with nothing but a Filofax and good intentions.

To the right, I saw a door with a small, filthy window and found a man sitting at his desk who looked vastly different from the sweaty workers in the warehouse. Most of the men wore suspenders with their guts hanging over their jeans. They sported different takes on mustaches and cowboy boots despite the ninety-degree Midwestern heat. No, this man was fiercely tan, wore a fake silk Versace shirt tucked into black slacks, and had gelled curly hair.

Like me, he also did not fit in at the warehouse. Unlike me, he seemed oblivious to this and fine with the arrangement. He had a box fan in the office, after all. This was no time to quibble about who went where. I needed experience on my resume other than Panera Bread Company, and this was my option.

"Chip? Hi, I'm Mora Thompson," I said, extending my hand for the second time that day. "We spoke on the phone. I'm your new intern."

"Hello, Mora! Welcome to your new career," Chip said with a white smile.

I looked around the cramped office. An oscillating fan gently blew glossy photos of him and a woman enjoying a fruity beverage on a boat. His bright Hawaiian shirt complemented his tanning bed glow. Stacks of paper held up a side table.

Shit.

* * *

I followed Chip around Springfield like a confused puppy. I was eager to learn but had no idea what I was doing. After several days, I realized Chip didn't know what he was doing either. That didn't seem to matter, though. He moved about town confidently, making people comfortable and saying anything that came into his head.

"Sure, buddy! Love that idea," said Chip. "It just doesn't fit into the strategic framework."

This strategy seemed to work because no one knew what *the strategic framework* was or where to find it. Inevitably, he continued about his business without addressing anyone's feedback.

I attended a jingle recording where I met Mike, my reference. He was in a band, had a great voice, and played a jingle he wrote for a local radio spot. I was thrilled to meet someone who created things that people produced. I peppered him with questions.

"How long have you worked in the industry?"

"Does the music come to you first or the lyrics?"

"Do you still play at the pizza restaurant on Fridays?"

Mike patiently answered my questions about the music business and showed me the initial project brief that inspired the jingle. After he gave Chip the final recording, Mike took his payment and ushered us out the door.

That's the biz, baby.

A few things became apparent after three weeks at Springfield Sabre.

1. Chip and the woman in the front office were seeing each other after hours. Her necklines continued to dip dangerously low. They made a cute couple, I guess?
2. Chip's tan was definitely not natural. I learned this because I was asked to manage his tanning bed appointments and pick up his favorite tanning oil at the salon.
3. Chip had little freelance work lined up after the radio spot.

After the jingle gig dried up, he decided I should try more business writing and less creative writing. This involved me sitting at a picnic table in the un-air-conditioned warehouse with only a Bic pen and a legal pad while trucks loaded and unloaded boxes of printers and copiers.

First, I wrote a memo to the office about a product launch delay due to supply issues.

Fine. I'm learning about the supply chain. Very client side.

Next, I wrote an email on Chip's behalf to the owner of the Springfield Sabre about office rent. The terms were fair, but he needed an extension.

Wait. He rents his office? I thought he worked for them.

But the pièce de résistance arrived one morning at the picnic table in a loosely closed accordion folder.

"Mora, this folder contains several years' worth of tax forms," he said, patting the folder. "For your next business writing assignment, I need you to review the documents and draft a tax abatement letter to the IRS."

Chip made this request without a hint of shame. His curls shone under the fluorescent lighting of the warehouse—dyed so black they were almost blue.

I had never filed my own taxes. I understood taxes as an abstract concept. I knew the king of England requested too many of them from the colonists. I knew they upset my father every March. I knew you should keep seven years' worth of statements in a file cabinet you bought, preferably, at a garage sale in the 1970s.

Beyond that, I had no idea what he was asking me to do. Ergo, I knew he should not ask me to do it.

"Sure," I said. "But since I know nothing about taxes, finance, or the IRS, would you kick off the document with a couple of bullet points?"

"Of course! I'll getcha started," he said.

So amiable! What a guy! Phew!

So I sorted his stack of highly personal financial information for the rest of the afternoon and drafted an abatement letter. I gave it to him before the close of business for his feedback.

"This looks great," he noted. "Couldn't have said it better myself."

I have no idea what I just wrote, and neither do you.

Was he as clueless as I was? Would either of us admit we didn't know what this meant?

"Great," I said. "I'll see you tomorrow."

Only, I didn't see him. I decided I would not return to my internship and mentor. I called Chip the next day and explained that until he had more specific promotional work, I was no longer comfortable supporting his business writing endeavors.

Two years later, when I applied to master's programs, Boston University asked me to describe my intern experiences in an essay. I couldn't lie. So I told the deans of Boston University's College of Communication every detail about my advertising internship and why working and going to school in Boston would be a great opportunity.

* * *

That November, I found myself at BU where I studied corporate public relations and was among twelve master's students who received the COM 101 Teaching Assistant position and scholarship. I settled into a chair in Associate Dean Tobe Berkovitz's cozy office on Commonwealth Avenue. "Tobe TV" was a political media master and advertising professor who loved vintage toys. He laughed when I spoke in a North Dakotan or Southern Missourian debutante accent and was fascinated by my father's ventriloquism hobby. We were weird.

"Tobe?" I asked one day while grading papers. "Why did you give me the COM 101 scholarship? You know my résumé is all on-campus extracurriculars. I know it's not the experience these other TAs have."

Tobe nodded. He was teasing me. I think.

"Well, we read your entrance internship essay, and I knew we had to get you the hell out of there. Also," he considered, "that essay was damn funny." More dramatically, he said, "I knew you were destined for greatness. Is that what you wanted to hear?"

"Yup. That was it." I continued grading papers and smiled, appeased.

"Do you have my notes ready for the O'Reilly interview?" he asked.

"Ugh, yes," I made a disgusted face and handed him a file. "Why do you continue to make appearances on that show? He's so condescending."

"Eh, it makes Mom happy to see me on TV," said the professor and expert in his field.

"Got it. Say no more," I replied.

We fell back into a comfortable silence. I graded papers, scanned the *Boston Globe*, and knew I was meant to be in that place at that moment.

Tobe got me. By sharing how I did not fit in and admitting the degree to which I could not and would not fit into the Springfield Sabre warehouse, I was fortunate enough to find those who celebrated my experience and perspective. He permitted me to stand next to people with perfect résumés, money to spare, convenient geographies, and designer clothes and say, "I may not fit in, but this is where I belong."

9.
KEEPING UP WITH THE SAMANTHA JONESES

Growing up, friends, family, and guidance counselors said I'd be great in public relations. I now realize no one knew what public relations professionals did. They explained public relations was a career path for those who had an aptitude for writing and relating to the public. Sadly, this was enough criteria (1) for adults to suggest it as a profession on career day, and (2) for me to consider it.

Based on movies and television shows, I knew public relations responsibilities might include: planning the Macy's Thanksgiving Day parade, defending the honor of President Bartlet, opening a public relations firm in London while living a parallel life, enduring a trial in broadcast news while sliding down a fireman's pole, and constantly wearing designer clothing. As you might guess, aside from what I learned in my degree program, my reference points for women in public relations and "PR life" included:

- Doris Walker, Maureen O'Hara's character from *Miracle on 34th Street* (Seaton 1947).

- C. J. Cregg, Allison Janney's character from *The West Wing* (Sorkin 1999–2006).
- Helen Quilley, Gwyneth Paltrow's character from *Sliding Doors* (Howitt 1998).
- Bridget Jones, Renée Zellweger's character from *Bridget Jones's Diary* (Maguire 2001).
- Samantha Jones, Kim Cattrall's character from *Sex and the City* (Star 1998–2004).
- Edina Monsoon, Jennifer Saunder's character from *Absolutely Fabulous* (French and Saunders 1992–2012).

While all these characters had flaws, they were self-assured, intelligent, and determined women who found their work fulfilling and exciting. Like them, I wanted confidence and creative flexibility. I wanted to say the right thing in uncomfortable situations. I wanted to win pitches and wow clients with brilliant ideas. I wanted to build trusted relationships with journalists and work with our design team to create award-winning concepts. Also, I wanted to wear an impeccably cut, fashion-forward suit that spoke volumes about my capabilities before I uttered a sound.

However, life did not imitate art. It turns out public relations professionals do a great job of making a tough gig look sexy.

After exploring copywriting in college, I began my public relations career in graduate school. I joined a creative event-planning firm with my friends to ease into the industry.

Just kidding. I dove in headfirst by cutting my teeth at a high-risk, low-reward boutique crisis communication and litigation firm. I worked with employers who juggled continuous catastrophes and managed lawyers, the national press, corporate executives, and local politicians.

My primary responsibility as the firm's public relations intern was to cut and paste relevant or placed media clippings into large three-ring binders. With their hodgepodge of magazine clippings, some binders' pages resembled murderers' and stalkers' ransom letters while others looked like depressing scrapbooks. What I would have given for a trip to Michael's and some glitter.

I decided crisis communications and litigation PR wasn't for me.

My second PR internship focused on fashion public relations. I joined a well-known underwear brand account that was experimenting with athleisure apparel. My supervisor gave me a key to the coveted "panty closet"—a great responsibility. As the panty closet gatekeeper, I organized underwear and athleisure clothing, coordinated panty pitch packages, and occasionally took home underwear samples with my supervisor's permission.

I called fashion magazine editors—always named Zoe—and asked if they would feature our underwear in their fashion magazines.

"Hi, is this Zoe at *Marie Claire*? Hi! It's Mora again. I am so sorry to bother you. I'm checking in to make sure you received the spring line of boy shorts I sent ... yes, they are *the cutest*. Totally ... cotton and modal..."

"Hi, is this Zoe at *Allure*? Hi! It's Mora. I'm making sure you received the tank tops I sent. Um, hello. I would be honored to send you more colors in the tanks. Yes, of course, you can layer the tank with gold jewelry and go out. Dress them up or down, I always say."

"Zoe at *InStyle*? Hi, this is Mora. Did you get the sample set of our new line I sent? Oh my gosh, that's great. Yes, of course, you can wear it at any age. Age is just a number, amirite?"

I'm not proud of it, but I thrived in this environment.

After graduate school, I returned to the Midwest and lived in Kansas City, Missouri, to be closer to family. There, I started my first full-time role at an international public relations firm.

I learned PR was not the glamorous career I saw in the movies or on TV. I wasn't C. J. or Bridget and certainly not Samantha. I worked about sixty hours a week. I rarely attended pitches, as I was too junior for new business meetings. When I conducted media relations, I cold-called the remaining journalists in the industry about agribusiness and nervously asked them if they heard the latest statistic about my clients' products—a task that made me feel like a telemarketer.

As for the impeccably cut, fashion-forward suits, I temporarily worked at Ann Taylor to afford my public relations career wardrobe, which consisted of poly-blend cardigan sets to seem like a confident corporate woman. I traveled internationally—to Canada. I maintain Toronto is one of the most beautiful cities in the world, but even my deeply rooted love for Anne Shirley from *Anne of Green Gables* could not keep me warm during a February trip to the Maritimes.

Without a panty closet to manage or Zoes to call, I felt lost and purposeless.

But unlike many graduates between 2005 and 2010, I worked in my chosen industry, which aligned with my degree, so I reminded myself I was fortunate. I was surrounded by capable, brilliant female professionals involved in the community, constantly innovating within the industry, so I stayed and pushed. I told myself to adjust.

I wrapped my poly-blend cardigan around my shoulders and went to work. This was my new normal.

* * *

I may not have been an official theater kid, but I gave Oscar-worthy performances at my public relations job.

One morning, tucked into a manager's office, we discussed the mounting stress from deadlines, due dates, and the upcoming holidays.

"I have to get back on the treadmill because I haven't been on it all week," she noted. "If I don't work out, I get totally insane." She shrugged.

"Wow. And that works for you?" I asked, fascinated that running in one place made someone feel less miserable and was not the source of misery.

"Well, I don't believe in medication for that sort of thing. If we take care of our bodies, they'll take care of us," she affirmed.

"Totally," I said. I already took my antidepressants that morning, so it was easier to be agreeable.

As a gal who was diagnosed with depression in high school, I didn't agree with her experience. I genetically inherited depression like an unwanted china pattern. When I was in the worst throes of a depressive episode, it was tricky to pull myself out of the fatigue fog and say, *Listen, self, it's time to hit the gym!*

I decided I would never mention stress management or mental health in front of my colleagues. The treatments I needed might involve low doses of involved pharmaceutical support, therapy, exercise, a creative project, rest, or a combination of the above to regulate how I showed up at work.

"Yeah. That's just . . . so important," I said. I reached for a generalized statement that was neither a lie nor the truth.

I tucked away the awareness that I needed to be mindful of my actions and attitude. The message I received was mental health could be willfully managed. I didn't question it. I didn't mention my concern to anyone. I didn't consider whether the conversation was appropriate. I didn't consider what worked for her might not work for me. Instead, I hoped I had enough discipline to manage my mental health in the future. At least enough to fool people at work.

Weakness was not a punishable offense, but it also was not rewarded.

* * *

In the cube next to me, I heard my colleague's desk phone ring.

"Hello?" said my colleague shakily into the receiver.

"Hi, Alexis. Can you come down to my office?" asked our vice president of human resources.

"Yes. I'll be right there," said Alexis, void of emotion.

Click.

I heard sniffles on the other side of our poorly constructed wall. A long exhale.

Should I say something? Should I let her be? I don't want to embarrass her. Damn. I love Alexis. She just got married, too.

I saw Alexis check her makeup in a compact, wipe her eyes, and walk down the hall. The rest of the day, I looked at my desk phone and waited for my call. I checked my voice mail and looked at the red light, waiting for it to blink. Whenever the phone rang, my heart stopped.

For the rest of the day, I watched colleagues receive the call, leave their desks—some took their bags and coats—and not return.

During the recession, being "good" was not necessarily good enough to keep a job. So I worked more. Within my company and the community, "the best" was the only acceptable outcome. I grew within the company and welcomed new leadership opportunities; however, that growth had a shadowy side.

I replaced fun activities like going to the movies with joining social organizations. My social interactions started to resemble business deals. If a date asked me what I did for fun in my spare time, I recited the extracurricular activities on my résumé like a robot wearing a red lip. I was one step away from asking my dates to sign a contract and notarizing it before we ordered dessert.

I joined boards and met other like-minded young professionals. Work blurred into my social life, and I felt pressure in both. My surroundings evolved from post-college scenes to professional environments. My peers had tabs at wine bars and mortgages in desirable neighborhoods. I bought more expensive clothes to attend cocktail parties and professional events. I moved into a trendy loft apartment in the arts district near pricey restaurants. I went into debt and lived a life I could no longer afford. I was terrified of failure and being a total fraud.

My health tanked. I worked during the day, went to board meetings, and then worked when I returned home at night. Anxiety bloomed in addition to depression. I went to the office with low-grade fevers. I assumed that was probably my body's normal temperature. My life was on overdrive—career, relationships, community, and travel accelerated toward an undefined destination. I sought perfection, and it eluded me.

What's going on? Samantha Jones never deals with this crap.

* * *

By 2012, my Oscar-worthy performances looked more like high school musicals. My pristine façade started to crack.

I looked exhausted and depressed. I have one of those faces that shows everything; it's inconvenient for client service, playing poker, and telling fibs. I completed tasks but felt emotionally and mentally disconnected from colleagues and friends. I avoided calling my family because it resulted in ugly sobs.

I was miserable at work, but I was equally afraid of being found out. I thought I'd be judged for poorly managing my mental health. For being weak. Unfortunately, my misery was misinterpreted as a bad attitude and lack of engagement.

After I spent several weeks wandering around like an extra from *The Walking Dead*, a manager called me into her office and asked me to shut the door.

This is a bad sign.

Not one to mince words, she got straight to the point.

"What is going on with you?" she asked.

I froze. I did not realize my performance had slipped that drastically. I definitely didn't realize she noticed it.

"You have a terrible attitude. I don't even recognize who you are anymore!" she said.

My shock morphed into shame as I internalized what she said.

How could I be so selfish? What was I thinking? This had to be my fault. Why couldn't I act happy? Why couldn't I *be* happy? Everyone else here seemed so put together. Why couldn't I fit in and be perfect too? Why wasn't I a person who could be perfectly happy?

Tears pricked my eyes and heat rose to my cheeks. I was afraid to open my mouth and say something I'd regret—something disrespectful or even more terrifying . . . the truth. I stared out the window.

"Are you listening to me?" she asked. "What were you thinking?"

"Yes," I said, nodding. "I heard you."

Her last statement ignited my own anger, and it bubbled and percolated to the surface, drowning my initial guilty response.

Where should I start? With my history of depression or the recent addition of anxiety? How my symptoms feel unmanageable? That I'm physically sick from this? That I sleep fourteen to sixteen hours a night every weekend so I can show up on Monday? That I'm terrified you'll find out and think I'm weak?

Instead, I pushed down my anger and tried to remain professional.

"I guess I wasn't thinking," I said. "I'll work on it."

I lied, but I could not muster enough energy for the truth. The truth was I *was* thinking. Constantly. I thought too much—about whether I pleased my boss, my clients, my parents, my friends, and my community leaders. I thought about having the perfect career, relationship, apartment, wardrobe, and social calendar. The pressure I felt to maintain this perfection was debilitating.

This isn't me. I don't belong here. All of this . . . feels wrong. My life shouldn't feel like this.

I left her office, walked into my own, and closed the door quietly. I rested my head on the cool desktop. My heart thumped, and I breathed deeply, trying to calm myself.

I heard colleagues chatter in the hallway and a printer buzz, but I felt worlds away. I was ready to move forward but needed a plan.

I turned on my computer, opened a Word document, and wrote the following list:

1. Fix situation with boss.
2. Break lease.
3. Sell unwanted things.
4. Find cheaper apartment.
5. Land new job.
6. Go on an adventure.

* * *

Two days later, I met with our general manager—the most patient and even-tempered woman I knew. I needed advice on how to manage... well... everything.

How could I balance my work schedule and have a social life? How could I meet everyone's needs and not feel stressed and sick all the time? How could I fix my relationship with my manager?

I sat in her corner office, which overlooked downtown Kansas City. I looked into her kind brown eyes and prepared my humble inquiry about managing up. Instead of speaking in a clear and collected manner, I burst into a tirade of hiccupy, snotty, and teary babble.

"What's wrong?" I sniffed, then hiccupped to punctuate each word. "I mean, I try, you know? It's, um, I work all the hours—a tissue? Sure. Thanks." I snuffled again.

My general manager's face expressed shock, concern, confusion, then concern again.

"Why don't you tell me what's happening here?" she asked calmly.

So I told her about the stress. I told her my manager approached me about it. I didn't say "mental health," but I was "working on things and getting help."

She listened. I used all her Kleenex. She nodded. I calmed down. I felt embarrassed about my outburst but relieved someone knew about my recent struggle. The most senior person in my office witnessed me at my worst, and I felt... free.

"I'm so sorry, but thank you for listening," I said. "I'll head back to my office." I threw my thumb over my shoulder, attempting to act casual again.

"Sure thing," she said. "And, Mora, there's nothing to be ashamed of."

I nodded and smiled.

Several months later, I prepared for a new role on the—*gasp*—client side.

I said goodbye to my fictional public relations muses: Doris, C. J., Helen, Bridget, Samantha, and Edina.

May your cosmopolitans be chilled, ladies.

* * *

Ultimately, being the picture-perfect public relations professional wasn't the perfect fit for me.

No matter how many meetings I attended or credit cards I opened, I never organized a Thanksgiving Day parade, lived a double life à la *Sliding Doors*, or participated in a *Sex and the City* designer clothing montage.

I wanted a new script and an original role. I wanted new characters, costumes, and a unique set design. Sure, the script and set design wouldn't suit everyone, but they'd be perfect for me—the new leading lady.

10.

THE JEFFERSON HOUSE

After leaving my public relations job and overpriced apartment, I moved into the Jefferson House, a bed-and-breakfast on Jefferson Avenue, in Kansas City, Missouri. At the Jefferson House, I lived with a stone-cold pack of misfits who, on the surface, made absolutely no sense. But this perfectly imperfect group of strangers became an impromptu family. We helped one another safely transition from one life phase into the next.

* * *

To reduce my debt and improve my mental and physical health, I would stop curating the life I thought I *should* have and create the life I wanted.

First, I needed a more affordable place to live. My loft apartment's once charming, exposed brick walls now felt heavy and prisonlike. I wanted a community and a comfortable place to hide away. I didn't visualize a specific floor plan or layout; instead, I focused on how I wanted to feel when I returned home.

I visited staged, overpriced developments downtown and realized the apartments I could realistically afford were on the brink of disaster. I needed a better real estate plan. Apparently, "manifestations of how I want to feel in my home" was not a search category on Apartments.com.

What am I doing? Focusing on how I want to feel in a home? What sort of flower child crap is this?

I rested my face in my hands and rubbed my eyes. I wearily looked up, prepared to close my laptop for the evening, and noticed a new Craigslist posting on the screen. My mom would be horrified that I was looking on Craigslist, but c'est la vie.

One Bedroom and One Bathroom Available for Rent in Historic Westside Home.

Top floor private bedroom and bathroom now available in a historic home located in Kansas City's Westside neighborhood. Homeowners, recently moved from Jersey (near France), are restoring home into a bed-and-breakfast. Room overlooks downtown art district and the new Kauffman Center for the Performing Arts. Shared living spaces and kitchen with two more housemates. Onsite and street parking. One block away from Westside restaurants, coffee shops, and new creperie. Serious inquiries only.

As a lifelong Anglophile, Francophile, and HGTV and home restoration enthusiast, I wrote the authors with an enthusiastic email. In less than an hour, Theresa Robinson, the homeowner, and I coordinated a house tour for that afternoon.

MY ROOM WITH A VIEW

The Jefferson House, an impressive three-story, nineteenth-century farmhouse, overlooked Kansas City's downtown. The stately home exhibited signs of the past fifty years of wear and tear. Mismatched, chipped paint covered the walls and dust occupied every shelf and mantle. Its steps and floorboards creaked like they were determined to live up to every gothic novel I'd read. Despite the years of neglect, the house stood on the precipice of a new adventure.

Theresa welcomed me into the dining room and sat at her antique kitchen table. Her spikey blonde hair stood on end, and she wore work boots, a sweater, and a long skirt. She made strong coffee in a French Press—so charming—and offered me cream. The rich coffee smelled like heaven, and I sipped from a smooth ceramic cup.

"I love these mugs," I admitted as I accepted mine.

"Oh! Yes, well. I made them. I'm a ceramics artist, actually. Can't wait to get my studio going. I miss working with my kiln." Theresa shrugged shyly and sipped her coffee. She spoke in a British accent, but I heard an American accent too. The combination was soothing—more *Masterpiece Theatre* than *Madonna*.

I never fell in love at first sight, but at that moment, I fell in love at first cup. I fell in love with Theresa Robinson, her ceramics, an old house, and the prospect of walking into an unknown adventure and accepting whatever outcome lay before me.

Welp, it's official. I'm one cup of French roast in and ready to throw down with anyone competing for my room at the Jefferson House.

I activated a full charm offensive.

I shared my vision with Theresa Robinson. I wanted to downsize and simplify. I said I loved the idea of a historical home and didn't mind the renovation process while I lived there. I loved being around creative people and projects.

Theresa shared her vision too. Theresa, a ceramics artist, and her husband Peter, a financial advisor, moved from Jersey to the United States. Their adult sons still lived in Britain, but Theresa and Peter needed a new adventure. The couple would restore, renovate, and open the Jefferson House, a local bed-and-breakfast in the Kansas City arts district. She worked part-time as a chef in a local restaurant but would spend most of her time renovating the home. She had room for two more tenants.

"Would you like to see the room? You can bring the coffee."

I clung to my ceramic cup. "That would be perfect, thanks," I said.

Room? What room? I only need to sit in this charming and cozy kitchen, drink coffee, and chitchat with you. That's it.

I almost forgot about my potential room. I would have signed papers based on her British accent and the antique marble tiles surrounding the fireplace.

We walked up two flights of broad steps to the top floor. On the landing, Theresa led me into a large room with a dark wooden floor, angled ceilings, and windows overlooking downtown Kansas City. The room looked worn but clean and included a closet and built-in space for more storage. I would have enough space for a bed, a sitting area, and a small coffee or tea station. I felt like a bird in her nest, cozily positioned high above the city.

"And the bathroom is across the hall," she noted. Opposite the landing was a small bathroom overlooking the garden with a pedestal sink and a large antique bathtub with clawed feet.

"No shower?" I noted doubtfully.

"No. Back at home, not everyone has showers in every bathroom, so I do forget," she admitted sheepishly. "We will add an attachment so you can wash your hair more easily." Quickly, she added, "I'll show you the rest of the house."

I easily forgot about forced bath time for the next six to twelve months when I saw the rest of the home. I saw a giant Viking stove and oven, pine cabinets that held her handmade ceramic dishes, and antique photos, prints, and art she planned to feature throughout the finished bed-and-breakfast. It was a warm mix of eclectic furnishings collected from experiences over time. Layers of well-loved antiques and modern art created an atmosphere that told a story about the owners. Nothing matched, but everything went together—a mix of old, new, created, and found.

"It's stunning," I said after the tour. "It's an enormous project, but your vision suits it perfectly. It reminds me of my parent's home where I grew up—my father's large paintings and my mom's organic textiles warming up the spaces. I like it when objects shouldn't fit but somehow belong."

"I can email you the contract today," Theresa responded.

"I'll send you a signed copy this evening," I promised, grinning like an idiot.

I moved into the Jefferson House one month later.

The Jefferson House included Peter, Theresa's husband, who pretended to be cantankerous but was charming as most English men are. Miriam, who was the same age as my younger sister, lived on the top floor of the house with me across the hall. Willful, funny, and kind, Miriam bounced around the house with big opinions and a soft heart. A young architect named Elvis also lived in the house. Ghostlike and quiet, he left and entered without anyone realizing it. Only Miriam and her elfin powers could get Elvis to engage with us. We hung on to that mystery man's every word when he did, hoping to glimpse what he did or thought.

Like any home, we had daily rhythms of going in and out independently to work, meeting friends, getting groceries, cooking, and repeating everything. I still missed showers but learned to love a long, hot bath. I bathed every morning before work, which became my favorite way to start the day.

The Jefferson House became a hub in a quirky, close-knit community. Miriam and I frequented the local restaurant where Theresa cooked as a sous chef in the evenings. We knew every dinner would also include a show and some banter with a local cast of characters.

"Oy, what's this, then?" said Peter when Miriam and I arrived at the restaurant. He typically stopped by on Friday and Saturday nights to chat with his neighbors and drink a glass of wine or two at the front bar.

"Put our drinks on his tab," we'd say loudly enough for Peter to hear, gesturing toward him.

"I'll add it to your rent," he'd say.

"Landlords these days!" I'd exclaim in mock horror.

The restaurant's head chef made traditional Spanish meals, tweaked local favorites with Castilian influences, and often cooked with wine. "Sometimes I put it in the food, too," she inevitably joked.

"Paella, bonitas?" she'd ask, emerging from a steamy kitchen, fragrant with saffron.

"*Sí*. Paella. Always paella," I said.

We ate the paella in the simple, tiny, and warm dining room decorated with twinkle lights and drank rounds of red table wine.

"Is this our life?" I asked Miriam as we walked back to the Jefferson House, laughing with flushed faces from too much wine and merriment.

After a year of Peter and Theresa's determination and hard work, the Jefferson House began to reveal itself. She was much more majestic than any of us realized. Richly-hued wallpaper covered the foyer when you entered the home. Each cleaned and polished wooden banister and door carving gleamed. Windows sparkled in the morning light and faded sunsets. The Robinsons bought beautiful beds for unused rooms in preparation for guests, and each was outfitted with soft but not fussy linens. The kitchen continued to be the heart of the home, where Theresa cooked meals that filled the house with scents I haven't experienced since. Spice mince pies at Christmastime, rosemary and mint throughout the summer, and roasted chicken and earthy soup throughout the fall and winter.

In a few short months, the Jefferson House was home.

Six months later, Elvis, Miriam, Theresa, Peter, and I planned a celebratory Christmas dinner before we traveled to see our separate family members for the holidays. We chose a date and time and prepared to eat in the newly furnished and festively decorated formal dining room. While Theresa played head chef, we all planned to have a role in preparing dinner—purchasing champagne and wine or cooking side dishes for the meal.

Elvis, Miriam, and I secretly planned a gift for Theresa and Peter. Miriam and I decided Elvis should conspire with us like little kids planning gifts for their parents and not twenty-something cohabitants planning a gift for their landlords. A day before our meeting, Miriam lingered for Elvis in the kitchen like an angry parent waiting for a kid who broke curfew. She reminded him of the next day's meeting when he returned from work.

"Elvis, you have to come. You promised." She folded her arms to look stern, but Miriam appeared impish when she wanted to get her way. The approach usually worked.

"I don't remember promising anything," Elvis noted, "but I'll be there." That was all the response we were to receive, so we accepted it and had faith he'd remember to join us.

The next day, Elvis, Miriam, and I met at the kitchen table at the assigned time to discuss our secret gift for Peter and Theresa. We chatted about antiques and locally made gifts, but, ultimately, we settled on something different.

"I have an idea." I stared at the kitchen table as I saw the gift come together in my mind's eye. "But, Elvis, you will play a key role in this gift. We can't do this without you."

"Like what?" Elvis looked dubiously at me over his Lucite glasses, but I could tell I piqued his interest.

"You're an architect. So you can draft and draw, right?" I smiled.

"Ooh." Miriam clapped her hands. I knew she liked that this was conspiratorial and collaborative.

"Great. We'll each need to play a part. First, Elvis, you'll need to—" As the group's lead bossy pants, I distributed responsibilities. Bowing our heads over notebooks, cookies, and coffee, we reviewed our plan's final details and agreed on the next steps.

This, we knew, was going to be good.

The evening of our dinner, we set the dining room table with candles, linen napkins, sparkling water, wine, and plates Theresa and Miriam prepared with holiday dishes. The room glowed with warmth in contrast to the dull gray day outside. We drank too much wine, and our stories became more animated. When we couldn't eat anymore, Theresa and Peter gave each of us gifts. They gave me Edward Gorey's poems because I loved the introduction to *Masterpiece Mystery!* on PBS. They also gave me a paisley potholder decorated in the Jefferson House's colors—a gift I still use today.

"We have something for you too. Elvis, do you have it?" Elvis excused himself and returned with an elaborately wrapped gift. Miriam beamed, as she had been responsible for wrapping it, which was done with her brand of flair.

"This is from us," Elvis said simply and gave the package to Peter.

Peter looked at each of us quizzically and raised an eyebrow.

"Should I be concerned? he joked.

"Probably." I nodded.

"Oh, Pete, just open it." Theresa rolled her eyes.

Peter unwrapped the package, and Theresa peered over his shoulder to view a framed image. The picture showed a cross-section of the Jefferson House, representing each of us as a vague figure in an architect's drawing going about our daily lives. I, naturally, bathed in my tub on the top floor. Peter sat in the sun in his garden. Theresa cooked in her kitchen. Elvis sat on his bed, and Miriam danced in her room. Elvis captured a unique moment in our lives with a few simple lines and shapes.

A moment in which—like the Jefferson House itself—we were emerging from the dust and transitioning from one phase of life into another. Peter and Theresa left Europe to open a bed-and-breakfast in the United States. I left a job and apartment to start a new career and reset my lifestyle. Miriam prepared for her new career in California.

Elvis . . . well, we had no idea what Elvis was up to but assumed he was on the brink of exciting new ventures.

"Right, then." Peter sniffed, but his eyes were teary as he looked at the gift. Theresa smiled at us and squeezed Peter's shoulders. Miriam, Elvis, and I exchanged glances.

As I said, we knew it was going to be good.

* * *

After years of stress and loneliness, I managed to find a community and create a family. Truthfully, the arrangement was complex to explain to most people—even my friends and real family. They thought I was crazy—selling furniture to live in "an attic," as some people dubbed it. Living in the Jefferson House became a turning point for me and my life. While there, I found a new job in health care. I worked with a kind and industrious group of people, and it was the happiest time in my career. That job eventually took me to Chicago, where I met my husband, David, on the first day in the city.

My true community organically formed when I followed curiosity and passion or found myself in a new circumstance and was open to new people. Brené Brown, our modern-day Mama Rumi, explains in her definition of belonging: "True belonging does not require you to change who you are; it requires you to be who you are" (Brown 2017).

Without realizing it, I found a family. At the Jefferson House, I didn't just fit in; I belonged.

11.

THE PLAN

Fast-forward eight years. It was 2021, and the world navigated a worldwide pandemic. I no longer lived a Bohemian adventure at the Jefferson House with Peter, Theresa, Miriam, and Elvis; I lived in Chicagoland with my husband, David, and dog, Watson.

David and I wanted to start a family, but we learned the process wasn't always as straightforward as it seemed.

THE BEST LAID PLANS
The events that occurred between 2019 and 2021 were not part of The Plan. For the uninitiated, allow me to introduce you to the finer points of The Plan.

The Plan is a specific set of life rules I believed would lead me to a happy and prosperous future. I diligently followed The Plan for years and was satisfied with its outcome. My life has always been fairly predictable, with a cause-and-effect pattern I could explain and manage with time, money, and determination. To deviate from The Plan meant I might delay goals, make compromises, or potentially, *gasp*, take a risk. Generally speaking, unacceptable behavior.

My story sounded similar to many of my friends. I went to school, earned good grades, attended a college with reputable programs for my specific skill set, then specialized in graduate school to ensure I received a job. I landed jobs at reputable companies to establish my career. Once established, I focused on climbing that proverbial corporate ladder—or lattice when I wanted to try something new. I dated different men and then met David, my husband. While dating, we lived in the city, ate at neighborhood restaurants, and went on vacations by Lake Michigan. We got engaged and moved into a condo just before the wedding. We had a traditional wedding in a Catholic church in my hometown with one hundred and fifty of our closest friends and family. We adopted a dog named Watson and moved into a white Cape Cod-style home in the Chicago suburbs. It was in a reputable school district, and we barbequed with our neighbors.

So far, The Plan had delivered on all fronts. Career? Check. Relationship? Boom. Friendships? Lifelong. I felt extremely fortunate and was ready to execute the next phase of The Plan. David and I wanted to start a family of our own. This didn't just involve having children; it involved forming new roles in our family and in our community. It involved us—a formidable family unit like the one I was part of growing up.

I can put down roots and belong somewhere. I will know who I am and what I should be.

Like me, many of our neighbors worked at one of our region's dozens of pharmaceutical or medical device companies. I'd carpool with other mothers and pick up lattes with them on our way to work. We'd go to the park and watch our kids play sports or perform at school plays. We would all be Cubs fans because we lived in the North Side of Chicago for so long. Our kids would have their first communion at the church up the street, but my girlfriends would understand my affinity for the occasional psychic reading and crystals. Our little family would visit Aunt Sarah and Uncle Jacob in the city and go shopping or out to lunch. I would enjoy a glass of chardonnay with the family on our porch on summer afternoons.

Did I picture myself in tennis whites and on vacations at five-star resorts? Sure. It's called manifesting. Besides, it worked with the Jefferson House.

I imagined The Plan vividly; however, in 2019, life events tested my faith, career, marriage, and sense of self. I learned The Plan was only an illusion, which turned my world upside down.

2019: NO PLAN

I sat at my faux mahogany work desk when David called me in a low and urgent voice. He explained he was driving from his mother's apartment en route to the hospital.

"What are you talking about? What happened?" I tried to make sense of David's story.

"My mom's neighbors called me. She hasn't been getting her mail or answering her door," he reported the events evenly and in a clipped voice, trying to communicate the circumstances as quickly as possible. He explained how he and his boss sped to her apartment, found her unconscious, and called the paramedics. Despite his protests, I left work and met David at the hospital.

There, we heard a series of phrases that did not compute. They included "lung mass," "brain tumor," and "immediate surgery." David's mother suffered from lung cancer that metastasized to her brain. She needed surgery to remove a brain tumor as soon as possible. Then, an oncologist would evaluate the lung cancer, give us a prognosis, and begin a treatment plan.

For the next nine months, David and I navigated a complex health care system and coordinated the appointments his mother needed during her surgical recovery and subsequent cancer treatments. Whether she recovered in a rehab center or our guest room, we suddenly oversaw every detail of her life.

During this chaos, David and I learned we were pregnant. Despite his mother's prognosis, we hoped a new grandchild would give her new life and hope. I felt nervous and thrilled about being pregnant. I immediately told my family, good friends, and colleagues. I also ignored the advice to wait to share the news until after the first trimester. I was tired of being sorrowful and wanted to feel and share joy.

However, the Saturday before Easter, I experienced pain and went to the emergency room. Doctors and nurses ran blood tests. One nurse held my hand while searching for a heartbeat on the monitor.

"I'm gonna squeeze your hand, honey," she said quietly. She squeezed as a technician searched for signs of life. I knew what the well-intentioned squeeze meant ... she should have seen the heartbeat by now.

To confirm, a young doctor sat next to my hospital bed and explained I was indeed pregnant, but my pregnancy would not be considered viable or result in a healthy birth.

"One more time?" I said, trying to wrap my head around this new narrative. I was pregnant but would not have a baby; I could expect a miscarriage within a week. The doctor also mentioned I might experience some discomfort and should "go home to relax."

Let me be clear: I did not relax, and it was more than *some* discomfort. Days of emotional turmoil followed by physical pain required another trip to the hospital for pain management and some serious therapy. The doctor's original advice made it sound like I would have a tough day, but a heating pad, Dove chocolates, and a couple of hours of Lifetime movies would fix me right up. I assure you; it was more involved than that.

After several weeks, I recovered and began to regain my strength. My body reset to its normal rhythms and sensations, but my mother-in-law's health declined as I recovered. That September, we said goodbye to David's mother after her fight with lung cancer. We grieved her loss and that brief expectation of parenthood.

That winter, we held on to a sliver of hope—it was the holiday season, after all.

"Surely," we toasted on New Years' Eve, "this year will bring us peace. To 2020!"

Cough.

Yes, I prayed 2019 was an anomaly and hoped David and I could refocus on healing, The Plan, and the next phase of our lives. Little did we know that a global pandemic was just around the corner.

2020: PLAN PIVOT

In 2020, I started a new job because I was eager for a fresh start. I learned my new company financially supported fertility treatments, which were prohibitively expensive. Leaving my previous role's safety, security, and happiness was difficult, but the previous year was so tumultuous, I didn't think a few more changes would be that impactful.

It was like laughing in fate's face and daring him to come and get me.

Within three weeks, I left a shiny new office and my new colleagues to work from home due to the COVID-19 lockdown. At the time, I thought things would return to normal in a few weeks, and my husband's insistence on buying giant packs of toilet paper from Amazon was a "let's head to our underground bunker and wait this thing out" mentality. But it became increasingly clear this pandemic would change everything, and no one understood the best way to manage our new reality.

Like everyone else, David and I felt isolated in our little world. We worked from home, ate at home, and watched the first season of *Love Is Blind* and *Tiger King* on Netflix. After several months, health care facilities opened, and we began our fertility journey. While life was stressful with a global pandemic and a new job, we reasoned we were at home and could support one another throughout the process. Plus, that biological clock is persistent, so there was no time like the present.

First, I tried all the less intrusive treatments, including three rounds of intrauterine insemination (IUIs). Despite being less intense, they still involved emotional ups and downs, medications, and weekly blood draws resulting in fatigue. After six months of unsuccessful treatments, David and I agreed to proceed with in vitro fertilization (IVF). People who have experienced IVF talk about the physical and emotional toll fertility treatments take on a couple, but I was determined to see the process through because that was part of The New Plan.

The process included daily hormone injections that drastically fluctuated my emotions and energy. This inevitably impacted my work and my relationship with David. David lived in a home he could not escape. In that home, our workdays blended with our personal lives, and I rode a constant roller coaster of hormones—crying about running low on disinfectant because we needed to disinfect the groceries when we got them.

"Don't we need to disinfect the groceries? Should we use disposable or cloth masks? How fast is Amazon Now? Can we get ice cream?" I asked.

"I'm going to play video games for a while," said David.

But we had hope. When we learned the recent round of IVF worked, and I was pregnant with a little girl, David and I were thrilled. We chose the name Lillian Marie Brinkman and referred to her by name. I followed every diet recommendation and wives' tale I could find that would ensure a safe pregnancy. I burned moxa incense, began acupuncture, swapped cosmetic products, ate organic food, and did everything possible to provide a positive pregnancy outcome. But Lillian had an irregular heartbeat at ten weeks, and our doctor was concerned. A week later, we went back in for a checkup.

Again, our doctor searched for a heartbeat but couldn't find anything. I experienced this once before. This time, David was with me during our appointment. I wish I could have saved him from the experience, but selfishly, I was grateful I wasn't alone.

"It looks like her heartbeat wasn't strong enough," our doctor said. "I can't detect anything now." She said this with empathy but didn't mince words.

Damn.

"But why?" I asked. For months, I diligently followed directions and took medications like clockwork. But no one ever explained why they never worked. They just expected me to move on to the next expensive solution. I repeated myself. "Why wasn't her heartbeat strong enough?"

"There could be a variety of reasons," she admitted. "We don't know which one it is." If I wasn't devastated, in a hormonal dilemma, and could think clearly, I might have asked follow-up questions; instead, I gave up on the conversation with my doctor.

"I see," I said.

I lied; I did not see. Nothing about my current reality made sense.

Let's break this down. I was isolated from my family and couldn't start my own. I went to work in my house. I wore a mask to Walgreens like a lazy ninja. I recently contemplated giving myself bangs based on a Pinterest infographic. Clearly, I was spiraling.

The Plan was failing, and I lived in an alternate reality with no control. The edges of the picture-perfect existence I could once see were now faded.

2020: UNPLANNED

In addition to the required social distancing, I separated myself more than six feet from my neighbors when I saw them. While they drank beer or wine and shook their heads at their kids' antics, I sipped on La Croix and steadied myself, trying not to envy their happiness. Being the only childless woman there, I felt ashamed, like I didn't fulfill some sacred obligation.

Does everyone think I'm childless by choice? Or I'm a career-obsessed woman who didn't want kids? Have I done enough with my career if I don't have kids? Have I plateaued?

I knew this train of thought wasn't productive. I also knew I spent way too much time in my head.

I became resentful. The pandemic had already kept me from my closest family and friends. Still, I felt further isolated from the women around me because I should not discuss my fertility journey if something went wrong. I quietly experienced infertility treatments like nefarious activities before work and on PTO days. In the waiting rooms, women avoided eye contact with one another, all while sipping on nonalcoholic drinks and searching for anti-nausea ginger candies at the bottom of their purses.

It felt bizarre and unbearably lonely, so I began discussing my fertility experience with people. I wanted them to understand why I was too tired to go out, avoided certain scents, stopped drinking alcohol, or had to leave for an appointment.

When I shared my fertility experience with other women, a new world—a sisterhood—blossomed. Women suddenly offered their fertility experiences—some in great detail—with generosity and vulnerability. My good friends, Jennifer and Jessica, who had difficult but successful IVF experiences, walked with me every step of my journey, sending texts when they couldn't hold my hand, reminding me I wasn't alone.

More surprisingly, neighbors shared their stories and offered advice, doctors' references, and support resources. A woman I randomly met shared her fertility story with me in her front yard. When I shared mine, she asked me to wait momentarily as she ran into her house. When she returned, she gave me a tiny wooden angel holding a child.

"She was my good luck charm during IVF," she said, placing the small figure in my purse. "Now she can be yours."

I avoided social media during the pandemic, but I began finding local women who shared advice about their experiences with doctors; what to expect with medication, insurance insights, recipes, acupuncture, and massage recommendations; and messages of celebration for good news and love and support for the bad news. A secret society of selfless women opened its doors to me, and I had never felt so held and embraced by a community before. I participated and shared in the community, too, offering knowledge where I could and providing information to women beginning their journey as I navigated the next steps of my own.

Yet again, the community and the perfect family unit I tried to curate was not my reality; however, when open, I unearthed a fellowship of empathetic women who showed me generosity, kindness, and bravery.

2021: THE NEW PLAN IS NO PLAN

By the summer of 2021, I no longer felt tied to The Plan. In fact, it looked unrealistic and one-dimensional. Sure, The Plan would have made things easier, but it didn't account for a global phenomenon and an unforeseen sisterhood.

Without The Plan, I hung on for dear life while keeping things in motion and ensuring my family's health and safety.

David and I pursued another round of IVF in early 2021. Unhappy at work, I began looking for yet another job. My parents required more help, so they moved to Chicago to be closer to my sister and me. I needed to find them a home and look for a new job, but that biological clock incessantly ticked, and our IVF coverage would only last so long. I knew deep down our lives were too stressful, and the weight of our careers, family planning, and caregiving might be too much. The stress of everything was impacting our marriage, and David in particular grieved the loss of the last miscarriage.

With nothing to lose—barring our marriage, financial stability, and sanity—we put our chips on the next round of IVF.

I underwent IVF treatments again while my parents lived with us. My mother suffered heart failure during this time, and we rushed her to the emergency room. She arrived at her new cardiologist just in time, began a treatment plan, and slowly healed. With the help of our neighbors, I found my parents a new home and helped them move blocks away from us.

While my parents lived with us and my mom recovered from heart failure, we learned we were again pregnant with another little girl. We were cautiously optimistic and hoped for a happy ending. I prepared for the first trimester symptoms I had experienced twice already.

* * *

Weeks later, I blinked and surveyed the sterile environment. I lay in a hospital bed under a scratchy sheet and avoided thinking about my recent loss.

My third pregnancy was my shortest, and I miscarried again.

An efficient, middle-aged nurse offered me juice and animal crackers. More like a little kid than a forty-year-old woman, I gratefully accepted the juice and snick snacks. When she left, I sat alone in a large room made for multiple patients.

Where's David?

Groggily, I looked for my husband but realized he wasn't allowed in the hospital due to COVID-19 restrictions. When the time came to walk out without a baby, David would pick me up and drive home, where we would once again attempt to reset our lives.

Where did I put my phone?

I looked for the device but realized I stashed it in a locker too far from my reach. I fell back onto my pillow, frustrated. I needed a distraction from the thoughts that kept threatening to creep into my brain. I didn't want to think about how excited I'd been the past three weeks. Or that I no longer understood my body's wants and needs due to fertility treatments. Was I hungry? Stressed? Thirsty? Hormonal? Who knows? I was a walking science experiment.

Instead, I tried focusing on a mauve-and-blue landscape painting created in a style favored by health care facilities nationwide. Then I looked at the hospital gown, my dry legs, and wool socks.

My God. What a depressing ensemble.

I would have expressed this to someone. I would have told David, my mom, or my sister that I felt void, separated from myself, and seriously needed updated athleisure wear.

"Yeah, it's pretty bad," someone would have said. Life would have felt more normal. Instead, I lost my baby during a pandemic and was alone. In times of tragedy, I find it helps to keep some things a touch superficial.

Slowly, the juice and animal crackers worked their magic. I edged out of bed, found a faded T-shirt and jean shorts in the locker, and dressed. I removed gauze bandages, tossed them in the trash, washed my hands, and threw cold water on my face. I brushed my hair and tied it back. David would be waiting downstairs, ready to take me home.

I checked out of the clinic and thanked the nurse. I decided at that moment I would not see her again. I was ready to close this chapter of my life. No more appointments, clinics, blood draws, injections, sonograms, hormones, and false hopes. I was so focused on this goal that I missed my husband.

I walked onto the brick pavement and felt the sun on my face. I saw David in our car in a nearby parking spot. He looked up from his phone and smiled as I approached. I climbed into my seat and enjoyed the blast of air conditioning. David leaned over, hugged me, and kissed my forehead.

"Are you okay?" he asked cautiously. He knew I might feel emotional. However, I felt more at peace than I had in several months. I was tired and uncertain about our future, but he waited for me. My family waited for me at home. We would eat lunch together. Everything would be fine.

"Yeah. I'm okay," I said, reaching over and squeezing his hand.

"Do you want to get an iced coffee?" he asked.

It's so nice to be seen.

David asked the perfect question. Weeks ago, I declared it the beginning of "iced coffee season," but I was pregnant and didn't partake in my favorite seasonal indulgence. David remembered because he is thoughtful.

We had empty agendas and uncertain futures, but at that moment, I had the best coffee date.

"Yes," I said, and smiled. "That sounds like a good plan."

12.
CONCLUSION

Twenty years ago, I wrote a "Forty Goals by Forty Years Old," list while nestled in a Starbucks booth in Springfield, Missouri. For tradition's sake, twenty years later, I sat at a Starbucks in Deerfield, Illinois, to write another list. Instead of wearing a gray Gap hoodie, I wore a camel knit turtleneck. Instead of sipping a Caffè Misto, I sprung for the Grande Latte—I earned it.

I wrote the list with the same heavy and black-inked yet fine-pointed Pilot V5 pen I used in college. The Pilot V5 is still my favorite pen for writing things of great significance. I planned to write many important things that day.

When I wrote my first list, I did so with a sense of urgency. I exported the list of goals from my brain to the journal, hoping to alleviate worry and document everything I should accomplish. Twenty years later, armed with my trusty Pilot and sitting cross-legged in my booth, I wrote more leisurely. I sipped coffee, wrote a line, crossed it out, checked Instagram, and rewrote the sentence. Sip. Write. Look outside. Lean back. Consider. Sip. Text. Write. And so on.

Eventually, only a few drops of lukewarm coffee sat at the bottom of my paper cup. My neck and lower back ached, so I twisted into a deep stretch and heard my back crack.

Yup. Definitely twenty years later.

I reviewed my scratchy cursive, psychological prose, and "Goals for the Next Twenty Years." I developed my new list of goals while keeping current criteria in mind. Was it a goal or a task? Was it motivated by an internal or external force? Was I achieving this goal for myself or someone else? I hoped to avoid old patterns of doing what I believed I should do instead of what I wanted to do—or forcing myself into a mold that may not fit me.

Was I older? *Yes.* Wiser? That's up for debate. The workaholic tried to creep into the exercise and distort it.

I could attribute metrics to these and gauge my success at a regular cadence—perhaps quarterly for the next two years to determine if I was moving the needle.

However, I didn't pursue those trains of thought.

Yikes. Why don't we put the quarterly review on hold for now? Okay, self?

I can tell you I felt calm, confident, and purposeful about my new list. If I followed through on these items, I knew I would have a vibrant and interesting life. I'd belong to a community filled with love, family, and friendship that motivated and nourished me. I would worry less about fitting in with others because I'd be content with myself. I knew it wouldn't be perfect—nothing is—but I could recover from life's hardships. I knew because I had already put them into practice—and they worked.

My list was as follows:

"GOALS FOR THE NEXT TWENTY YEARS"
- Enrich your daily life with art, theater, music, comedy, reading, or writing.
- Live near, be in, sail on, lie by, and drink more water.
- Focus on your goals and not someone else's success.
- Look for, and listen to, the outliers. Learn from them.
- Share your untold stories; they're more common than you think.
- Create the role you want.
- Develop communities, not lifestyles.
- Go on adventures but remember to find beauty where you are.
- Love your family—whatever its shape or size.

My list is specific to me; however, I urge you to create your own. Create a list capturing small, everyday miracles and stretch goals that embody you and your off-kilter, on-brand, glorious, weird, nuanced, complicated self. Revisit, update, and celebrate the list's contents. Sit with it. Sink into it. Then—here's the most important part—live it.

When I did, my life shifted. My world felt more . . . me. I met new people, began creative projects, recognized professional opportunities, traveled, reconnected with old friends, and met new ones. I wasn't an outsider looking in. I wasn't different, less worthy, strange, or unlovable. I was the heart of a new world that reflected my authentic self. I belonged because I could just be.

Being me, it turns out, is pretty great.

ACKNOWLEDGMENTS

I could not have written this book without the space and support of my family. Mom, simply put, you show me what strength and love look like every day. Dad, thank you for modeling creative vulnerability throughout your career. As an adult, I now realize how brave that really was. Sarah ('Ister), thank you for years of storytelling, make-believe, pretend, play, lookbooks, and long talks. They still sustain me. Jacob, I'm in awe of your determination, but nothing eclipses your kindness. Mom Mom and Pop Pop, you inspire some of our family's best stories.

Thank you to my friends and beta readers, Jennifer Jones, Nicole Chilton, Cristen Jester, and Jon Gray, who provided thoughtful and valuable feedback within a tight timeline.

Terry McDougall, thank you for helping me make the right connections. First emotionally, then socially.

Thank you to my editorial team, Katie Sigler, Jen Wichman, and Carol McKibben, for bravely wading through the editorial waters with me. Jacques Moolman, you are a rare unicorn-like combination of marketing expertise and sage advice.

Thank you, Jessica St. Clair, June Diane Raphael, Casey Wilson, and Danielle Schneider, my dear podcast friends I never met, for inspiring me to find my voice. Thank you for blending humor with vulnerability and generously sharing yours.

Author Community, this dream would not be a reality without your support. They say it takes a village. I'm so glad you are in mine.

Chris Anderson	Valerie Conners
Isa Bank	Ross Cully
Kathleen Bauer	Katie D'Angelo
Jenelle Beavers	Janis Dezso
Marisa Benjamin	Stephanie DiVito
Tobe Berkovitz	Jessica Dorzinsky
David Borsheim	Cory Ezell
Amanda Braderick	Rizwan Farooqui
David Brinkman	Michael Farrington
Lindsay Brown	Melanie Fayta
Phil Brown	Heather Field
Tracey Burmeister	Aaron Fox
Michael Bushert	Shannon Franco
Patricia Carroll	Ann Friedman
Carlos Casas	Mitch Fuqua
Jessica Charlsen	Dan Gedman
Nicole Chilton	Colleen Glynn
Meredith Coburn	Susan Gottschall
Jay Collins	Jon Gray

Rick Gray
Dahlia Hanin
Mary Hannon
Sharon Harper
Desarae Harrah
Chad Harris
Ronda Harris
Suzanne Hatcher
Bryan Hayes
Tara Hefner
Lindsay Heyer
Monica Higgins
Angela Hollen
Stephanie Hornickel
Kelli Huddleston
Elizabeth Hutson
Larry Jacob
Jenny Jansen
Sheila Jansen
Cristen Jester
Jennifer Jester
Nancy Jester
Elizabeth Johnson
Jennifer Jones
Jennifer Jordan
Kurt Kapfer
Dan Kiggins
Eric Koester
Sarah Kover
Jennifer Kraenzle
Anna Kroner
Ericka Labedz

Jordan LaBelle
Erin Lanoue
Michael Larkey
Evelina Leece
Jennifer Lerner
Barry Loudis
Andy Maggard
Mark Malin
Catie Malooly
Terry McDougall
Jessica Merino
Lina Midla
Susie Morris
Kristen Motsenbocker
Susan Mueller
Shawna Nagel
Tracy Nielsen
Christy Noland
Melissa Novak
Liz Olson
Frankie Oviedo
JoAnne Parker
Gina Parsons
Janna Pattison
JC Perez
Monica Philips
Raquel Pichardo
Allison Pickering
Katie Proctor
Angie Rataj
Nicolle Ratliff
Olivia Ring

Joshua Ruwet
Micha Sabovik
Tommy Schenck
Erin Schwarz
Ashley Searcy
Andrea Sifferman
Ashley Silverman
Marshall Stanton

Kathy Steinmetz
Stepheny Stordahl
Sarah Thompson
Wade and Maureen Thompson
Laura Westbrock
Annie White
Sarah Williams
Hugo Xi

APPENDIX

2. PHYSICAL EDUCATION

Boyle, Robert H. 1955. "The Report That Shocked the President." *Sports Illustrated* Vault. August 15, 1955. Accessed March 16, 2023. https://vault.si.com/vault/1955/08/15/the-report-that-shocked-the-president.

Edwards, Phil. 2015. "A Brief History of the Bizarre and Sadistic Presidential Fitness Test." *Vox.* April 24, 2015. https://www.vox.com/2015/4/24/8489501/presidential-fitness-test.

3. LITTLE MEN

Vanity Fair. 2016. "The Photo That Changed Candice Bergen's Life." *Vanity Fair.* February 4, 2016. Accessed March 16, 2023. https://www.vanityfair.com/hollywood/2016/01/candice-bergen-charlie-mccarthy-photo.

7. LATE BLOOMER

Abrams, J. J., and Matt Reeves. 1998–2022. *Felicity*. Filmed in New York City, New York. Television Series, 42–45 minutes. https://www.imdb.com/title/tt0134247/.

Wolf, Dick. 1990–Present. *Law & Order*. Filmed in New York City, New York. Television Series, 40–44 minutes. https://www.imdb.com/title/tt0098844/.

8. HOMETOWN INTERN

Krasinski, John. 2010. "Sabre—The Office." Filmed February 4, 2010 in Panorama City, California. Television Series Episode, 30 minutes. https://www.imdb.com/title/tt1564720/.

9. KEEPING UP WITH THE SAMANTHA JONESES

French, Dawn, and Jennifer Saunders. 1992–2012. *Absolutely Fabulous*. Filmed by BBC Productions in Europe. Television Series, 30–60 minutes. https://www.imdb.com/title/tt0105929/.

Howitt, Peter, director and writer. 1998. *Sliding Doors*. Filmed by Intermedia in London. Film, 99 minutes. https://www.imdb.com/title/tt0120148/.

Maguire, Sharon, director. 2001. *Bridget Jones's Diary*. Filmed by Universal Pictures in London. Film, 96 minutes. https://www.imdb.com/title/tt0243155/.

Seaton, George, director. 1947. *Miracle on 34th Street*. Filmed in New York City by Twentieth Century Fox. Film, 96 minutes. https://www.imdb.com/title/tt0039628/.

Sorkin, Aaron. 1999-2006. "The West Wing." Filmed September 19, 1999 to May 14, 2006 in Burbank, California, Washington D.C. metro, Canada and Los Angeles. Television Series, 44 minutes. https://www.imdb.com/title/tt0200276/.

Star, Darren, director and creator. 1998-2004. *Sex and the City*. Filmed by HBO Entertainment in New York City. Television Series, 25 minutes. https://www.imdb.com/title/tt0159206/.

10. THE JEFFERSON HOUSE

Brown, Brené. 2017. *Braving the Wilderness: The Quest for True Belonging and the Courage to Stand Alone*. New York: Random House.